DARK GRANITE AXE, LENGTH 9½ INCHES, WEIGHT 4¾ POUNDS.
LAPEER COUNTY.

PRIMITIVE MAN IN MICHIGAN

By
W.B. HINSDALE

Published
by
Avery Color Studios
AuTrain, Michigan 49806

ISBN - 0-932212-33-6

Printed - April 1983

Primitive Man In Michigan was first published in 1925 by the University Museum, University of Michigan. Their Permission has been granted for this reprint.

CHIEF LITTLE ELK

DEDICATED
to

This reprint of *The Primitive Man In Michigan* is dedicated to Eli Thomas, Chief Little Elk, leader of the Chippewa tribe with headquarters at Mount Pleasant on the Saginaw Chippewa Isabella Reservation. Chief Little Elk has devoted his life to teaching young and old the ways and beliefs of the Indian and the colorful history of his people.

PREFATORY NOTE

The Michigan Handbook Series has been initiated for the purpose of presenting summaries of the botany, zoology, anthropology and geology of the state for the use of teachers, students and others interested in the natural sciences.

The numbers are not to be technical contributions nor popular accounts, but rather of the nature of elementary reference books and introductions to the study of individual groups and sciences, as these are represented in Michigan.

ALEXANDER G. RUTHVEN

ACKNOWLEDGMENT TO SUPPLEMENTARY INTRODUCTION

As publishers of this reprint we wish to express our thanks to James J. Krakker for his months of research and work in the preparation of this introduction.

James Krakker has long had an interest in Michigan archaeology. He pursued graduate studies at the University of Michigan. His dissertation research concerned the lifeways and social organization of late prehistoric societies in southeast Michigan, however, his interests include all phases of prehistory and also extend to the historic Euroamerican occupation. Since the 1960s he has participated in field work in Michigan and elsewhere in the Midwest as well.

JAMES J. KRAKKER

CONTENTS

CHAPTER VII

Hunting. Agriculture. Trade and Commerce. Warfare.
Carpentry. Clothing. Medicine. Perforation of Skulls.
Caches. Domestic Life. Rock Carvings.

CHAPTER VIII

Flints. Axes, Celts. Ceremonials. Clubs. Gorgets. Pipes.
Mortars and Pestles. Pottery. Copper.

CHAPTER IX

SUPPLEMENTARY INTRODUCTION
By J.J. Krakker

Contributions Of Wilbert B. Hinsdale
To Michigan Archaeology

Primitive Man in Michigan has been a widely read introduction to Michigan prehistory. Since it was published in 1925 much has been learned about Michigan prehistory. Advances in Michigan archaeology have been too extensive to review in a few brief pages. The reader should refer to publications listed below as suggested further reading. Nevertheless, *Primitive Man in Michigan* has an important message for the modern reader. In particular, Hinsdale's concern about the preservation of Michigan prehistory remains as important today as ever. Furthermore, *Primitive Man in Michigan* is only one of Hinsdale's important contributions to the development of Michigan archaeology. To be appreciated Hinsdale's contributions need to be considered in the context of the archaeological theory and problems of his active years during the 1920s and 1930s.

Primitive Man in Michigan was published early in Hinsdale's archaeological career. The book is, therefore, a better introduction to than a summary of his work. Interests evident in it are more fully elaborated in his later works and by later investigators. Archaeology was only one aspect of Hinsdale's anthropological inquiries. In *Primitive Man* and his other works Hinsdale placed Michigan prehistory in an anthropological perspective.

HINSDALE AND HIS WORKS

Hinsdale's archaeological career is an interesting one. He was not by profession trained as an archaeologist; in fact, formal training in North American archaeology as a profession became available long after Hinsdale's education was completed. He was professionally a physician and only by avocation an archaeologist.

Hinsdale was born in 1851 in Wadsworth, Ohio near Akron. He graduated from Hiram College in 1875. In 1887 he received a medical degree from the Homeopathic Hospital College of Cleveland and later served on the staff of that institution.

In 1895 Hinsdale came to Ann Arbor to become Dean of the School of Homeopathic Medicine as well as director of the homeopathic hospital and a professor. He joined his brother Burke A. Hinsdale at the University of Michigan who was the professor of the science and art of teaching from 1888 to 1900. Both brothers had an interest in history. Wilbert Hinsdale transferred an early interest in archaeology from Ohio to Michigan. No doubt his teaching and administrative duties limited the time he could devote to archaeology. However, somehow he found the time to pursue archaeology soon after his arrival in Ann Arbor. His investigations in the vicinity of Ann Arbor are reported in an article in the Washtenaw Times in 1901.

In 1922 Hinsdale retired and was appointed Custodian in Charge of the Collection in Michigan Archaeology and was Associate in Charge of the Great Lakes Division within the newly organized Museum of Anthropology under the direction of Carl Guthe. Hence, at the age of 70 Hinsdale was free to devote full time to his avocation.

Primitive Man, published soon after his retirement, was only the beginning of a productive career as an archaeologist and anthropologist. He published papers in the Papers of the Michigan Academy of Science, Arts and Letters and elsewhere between 1925 and 1941. His other major and most widely known works today are the *Archaeological Atlas of Michigan* (1931b) and *Distribution of Aboriginal Population in Michigan* (1932a). *The First People of Michigan* (1930b) aggregated some of his papers published earlier, but seems little read today. Another smaller publication of local interest is *Indians of Washtenaw County* (1927b) which presented for one county the type of information that was compiled for the whole state in the *Atlas.*

RESEARCH AND PRESERVATION LINKED

Primitive Man was intended as an introduction to Michigan archaeology for the general public. The book was motivated by Hinsdale's desire to preserve archaeological remains and to direct interest in archaeology in a constructive direction. He recognized that the archaeological record is fragile, but believed that the key to preservation was education. The book was issued as the first volume in the Michigan Handbook Series of the University of Michigan Museums. The intent of the series was not to provide popular accounts, but elementary introductions and references to the study of natural sciences in Michigan.

In the introduction Hinsdale urged the initiation of an archaeological survey of Michigan. An archaeological survey consists of systematic recording of archaeological information and compilation of a site inventory. He was not the first to suggest such an endeavor. Harlan I. Smith, a native of Saginaw who became an eminent North American archaeologist advocated a state survey at the turn of the century. In spite of Smith's efforts no permanent state survey was established. Nevertheless, Smith did compile an inventory of the then known sites in Michigan.

Later, in 1922 George Fox reviewed the status of archaeological research and knowledge in Michigan. He urged the formation of a state survey and archaeological society (Fox 1922).

By the 1920s many states had societies or state agencies devoted in whole or part to the protection and investigation of archaeological remains. Hinsdale devoted himself to the task of archaeological survey and preservation in Michigan.

Aside from a purely scientific interest in systematic description and collection of information, the need for a survey was consistent with Hinsdale's concern with preservation of Michigan prehistory. A site survey would be a useful initial step toward a preservation program. Later in Chapter II (p. 29) Hinsdale argued that preservation of archaeological remains is a duty of the state.

On the first page of the introduction Hinsdale invited the assistance of others interested in Michigan archaeology for the purposes of an archaeological survey and the preservation of Michigan prehistory. Hinsdale realized that both goals required cooperation and widespread public support. Indeed, over the years he conducted a voluminous correspondence. The acknowledgments include many individuals, among them George Fox of Three Oaks and Dowagiac, Fred Dustin of Saginaw, Walter Schmidt of Pinconning and Edward Stevens of Kalamazoo. They, among others, assisted in the compilation of the *Atlas,* helped to establish a state archaeological society and made scholarly contributions to the study of Michigan prehistory in their own right.

Hinsdale's willingness to work with others is shown in his participation in the foundering of the Michigan Archaeological Society in 1924. The society integrated the efforts of members for the compilation of archaeological information (Stevens 1927). In addition, Hinsdale also promoted the educational functions of the society. The society disbanded during the depression, but was reorganized in 1949.

Hinsdale's interest in preservation of Michigan prehistory also extended to legislation to protect archaeological remains. Hinsdale was instrumental in enactment of state legislation in 1929 to protect antiquities. Efforts toward preservation have continued. Since 1972 the Michigan History Division of the Michigan Department of State has taken an active role in the administration of archaeological survey and preservation. Today federal enactments require evaluation and salvage of cultural resources as part of the environmental impact review process for federally funded or licensed projects.

ACTIVE YEARS

The 1920s and 1930s were active years for archaeological and ethnographic field work in Michigan by the newly formed Museum of Anthropology. Hinsdale, in spite of his advanced age, was active in both. Others on the Museum staff including Emerson F. Greenman, Frank Vreeland, Vernon Kinietz, George Quimby and Carl Guthe were engaged in field work throughout the state.

The outcome of Hinsdale's survey was the *Archaeological Atlas of Michigan.* Without doubt, the *Atlas* was Hinsdale's most time consuming project during his archaeological career. He began collecting information soon after retirement and the volume was published as number four in the Michigan Handbook series in 1931. The format of the *Atlas* is modeled after the *Archaeological Atlas of Ohio* compiled by William C. Mills and published in 1914.

Although Hinsdale gleaned information from documentary sources the survey was by no means an "armchair" endeavor for him. Hinsdale traveled thousands of miles around the state to visit sites, talk to informants and conduct small excavations. Some of his excavations are reported in the Papers of the Michigan Academy of Science, Arts and Letters. Although not all the sites recorded in the *Atlas* were examined by the Museum's staff, the *Atlas* does represent a compilation of the information available at the time and remains a useful reference to this day.

Even after publication of the *Atlas* Hinsdale remained active. He continued to visit sites and conduct brief excavations until the mid-1930s. He visited the Younge site in 1934 where in 1935 Greenman conducted the most extensive excavation in the state up to that time. Emerson Greenman became Curator of Great Lakes Archaeology in 1935 and began three active field seasons in Michigan before turning his attention to Manitoulin Island and study of the historic contact period and geochronology.

Hinsdale's activity seems to have declined in the mid-1930s. Old age must have been overtaking him, although he lived until 1944.

BEGINNING OF AN ECOLOGICAL VIEW

The effort devoted to compiling the *Atlas* led to more than simply an inventory of Michigan archaeological sites. Hinsdale became concerned with the explanation of the observed distribution and density of sites. Perhaps this interest was an outgrowth of the perception that there is a relation between culture and environment briefly mentioned at the end of chapter II of *Primitive Man* or, perhaps, resulted from the influence of Melvin Gilmore, an eminent ethnobotanist who joined the Museum of Anthropology staff in 1929.

The beginning of an ecological approach is seen in his article "Indian Corn Culture in Michigan". Here Hinsdale brought together documentary evidence and direct observations on the size and distribution of Indian corn fields marked by distinctive corn hills. Hinsdale concluded that corn cultivation was an important and widespread subsistence activity for the prehistoric inhabitants of the lower peninsula. He also made observations about the relation of agriculture to both the physical and social environment. He suggested that pine-dominated areas would not have been suitable for pre-

historic cultivators anymore than for more recent Euroamerican cultivators. In addition, he suggested that the impact
of European demand for furs shifted Indian economic effort
away from cultivation to hunting.

A more fully developed ecological discussion emerged in
the *Distribution of Aboriginal Population in Michigan.*
Here Hinsdale considered the distribution of subsistence
resources in more detail. He related the distribution and
density of resources to the distribution and density of prehistoric population indicated by the pattern of sites. Later,
in the 1960s investigation of human adaptation in an ecological
context became a major focus of Michigan archaeological
studies.

PROBLEMS OF NEW WORLD SETTLEMENT,
STRATIGRAPHY AND CHRONOLOGY

The first three chapters of *Primitive Man* place Michigan
prehistory in the wider perspective of New World prehistory
and anthropology. Hinsdale grappled with the problem of
the antiquity of human occupation in the New World.

The antiquity of the arrival of people in the New World was
vigorously debated at the time (Willey and Sabloff 1980:
46-50, 121-123). While Hinsdale correctly placed the presence
of people in the New World at the end of the Pleistocene (the
last glacial period), he expressed caution about the length of
human occupation of the New World since various claims for
great antiquity had been demonstrated to be unfounded
(Holmes 1919; Hrdlicka 1907). However, later in the 1920s
finds of chipped stone tools embedded in the bones of extinct
Pleistocene animals on the Great Plains established without
doubt the association of people with Pleistocene animals and
a human presence in the New World at the end of the Pleistocene.

The date of the end of the Pleistocene remained uncertain

until more recently. The development of radiometric dating techniques, most notably radiocarbon dating, has established a minimal age for the arrival of man in the New World of about 12,000 years ago.   There remain claims of greater antiquity of New World settlement, but the evidence is still ambiguous.

Hinsdale's discussion of Dixon's method in Chapter I refers to a book then recently published (Dixon 1923). Although physical variation in New World populations is evident, Dixon's reconstruction of migrations based upon the idea of fixed racial types defined by head shape is of little repute today. His assumptions and methods were questionable even at the time (Boas 1923).

The mention of stratigraphy in the second chapter indicates the difficulty at the time of reconstructing cultural change through time in the prehistory of Michigan. The book was written at a time when stratigraphic evidence of cultural changes through time was beginning to accumulate in the Southwest and coastal areas (Willey and Sabloff 1980: 55-57, 84-93). Chronology can be obtained from stratigraphy because sequential deposits indicate the order of events and therefore provide evidence of cultural changes. Long depositional sequences as in coastal shell middens or caves and rock shelters are unavailable in Michigan, therefore, clear evidence of changes in culture through time was not immediately apparent in Hinsdale's time. In this regard, Hinsdale distinguished the modest-sized mounds of Michigan which are artificially constructed mortuary monuments from the midden mounds consisting of accumulations of refuse at intensively occupied habitation sites common along the coast and major southeastern United States rivers.

A major advance since the writing of *Primitive Man* has been the increased knowledge about the sequence of changes in cultural adaptations and environmental changes that occurred over the last 12,000 years in Michigan. By contrast, Hinsdale was able to say little about prehistoric cultural changes indicated by the archaeological record, although by most definitions archaeology is concerned with the sequence of past events, cultural changes through time and how changes can be explained (p. 28, 34). Hinsdale was well aware that people were in the New World thousands of years before the arrival of Europeans, and by implication in Michigan, but he had hardly a clue about the relative ages of features and sites. Likewise, changes in the environment since the end of the glacial period had not been reconstructed.

Evidence of vegetation changes consists of pollen sequences preserved in sequentially deposited sediments of bogs and lakes within the Great Lakes region. Study of the stratigraphic pollen record began in the Great Lakes region in the 1930s. Although pioneering work by geologists reconstructing the late glacial and post-glacial changes in the shorelines of the Great Lakes had been done, Hinsdale does not mention these changes. Beginning in the late 1930s geochronology and cultural relations became a focus of research. Today with a more complete understanding of environmental changes the interpretation of prehistory has become both more complex and interesting than Hinsdale could have known.

The third chapter consists of definitions of terms used in the book. In keeping with the introductory intent of the book Hinsdale defined some general anthropological concepts and usages that would be unfamiliar to readers outside of archaeology or anthropology.

THE ARCHAEOLOGICAL RECORD IS FRAGILE

Chapter IV is the most important one for the modern reader. Hinsdale explained that archaeological remains are the record of the past. Even today the record is still incompletely understood. The archaeological record is fragile since remains are at or near the ground surface and even shallow ground disturbance can be destructive.

Hinsdale rightly noted that the archaeological record consists of far more than objects alone; the context of objects and the relation among objects carry important information. Once objects are removed from their original context their original provenience must be preserved with written records. To remove objects from the surface or ground without documentation is simply to tear pages out of the record of prehistory.

Hinsdale made the point that the goal of archaeology is the accumulation of knowledge about the past, not simply the collection of objects. Excavations are conducted not simply to recover objects, but to study their context and relation to other objects. Professional training is necessary to make the proper observations and records essential for scientific analysis.

SITES, ARTIFACTS AND ANTHROPOLOGICAL INQUIRY

The remaining chapters discuss site types, features, artifacts and less tangible aspects of prehistoric activity. Perhaps earthworks discussed in Chapter V are the most obvious site type and attract the most attention from the general public. Hinsdale lamented their destruction. Agricultural activities had by the early 20th century leveled many of the earth enclosures visible to pioneers. Since earliest Euroamerican settlement mounds had been the target of the shovels of curiosity seekers. Hinsdale had a particular interest in mounds and enclosures. Much of his field work, beginning in 1923, was devoted to their investigation (1925a, 1929b, 1930a). Likewise, his colleagues, Dustin and Greenman, also gathered information from extant earthworks (Greenman 1926, 1927; Dustin 1932).

In chapters VI attention turns to trails and other site types. Hinsdale had a great interest in trails and travel. He considered routes of water travel more fully in a paper published in the Papers of the Michigan Academy of Science, Arts and Letters (1927c). He noted that General Land Office notes made during the original land survey in the 19th century and early maps would be useful sources of information for Indian trails. These sources had already been utilized by Edward Stevens (1927) in Kalamazoo County. Hinsdale and Stevens expanded coverage to the whole state and trails are prominently featured in the *Atlas.*

The scant attention given to site types other than earthworks should not be taken as an indication of low scientific potential in comparison to earthworks. Knowledge and analytical methods were unavailable to Hinsdale for him to appreciate the record of activities contained in the remains of ordinary habitation sites. Every site has a story to tell. Hence destruction of any site, not just the largest or most remarkable, diminishes the record of the past.

Chapter VII discusses less tangible aspects of aboriginal life. Although by today's standards the treatment is rather conjectural, it is of interest because it shows the broad archaeological and anthropological perspective Hinsdale was developing. Hinsdale drew widely on archaeological and anthropological literature available to him at the time to elucidate various aspects of aboriginal activity in Michigan. Several of the topics became the subject of later publications, where Hinsdale's interest ranged beyond strictly archaeology to other concerns about aboriginal life in Michigan.

Among the topics discussed is medicine. No doubt, being a physician Hinsdale had an interest in native pharmacy and curing techniques. He devoted time to collecting information on native medical practices and beliefs in the later 1920s.

Both in relation to curing and in his earlier definition of

culture (p. 25) Hinsdale made brief note of religion, ritual and beliefs. Later works show Hinsdale was very much interested in aboriginal ideology (1926b, 1930b, 1931a, 1932b).

Another topic Hinsdale discussed is skull perforation. Again Hinsdale's background in medicine probably attracted his attention to the practice of skull perforation earlier observed in Michigan (Gillman 1875; Starr 1890). Trephination is a surgical technique used to treat head injuries and other distresses. Hinsdale believed that he had found a true case of trephination because there was evidence of healing. However, the practice of skull perforation in Michigan seems to be part of a post-mortem practice including skull perforation or plaque removal and modification of long bones probably related to mortuary ritual. Hinsdale suggested that skull perforation would be an interesting topic for study and he published several papers on occurrences of skull perforation (1925b, 1934; Hinsdale and Greenman 1936; Hinsdale and Cappannari 1941).

Next, in chapter VIII Hinsdale described various artifact forms found in Michigan. Descriptive typology depends on the purpose of analysis and purposes have changed through time. Today emphasis is on function and stylistic variability.

In the 1920s description of traits including material items or attributes of items and less tangible cultural practices were the basis of the definition of culture areas. Cultural core areas were defined by the areal distribution of specific traits. Change of culture through time was described in terms of diffusion of traits among culture areas. There was little concept of cultural stages as changes in cultural adaptation as now defined. In the 1920s the sequence of cultural changes that occurred since the end of the Pleistocene was only beginning to be realized. In the 1930s descriptive typology became more systematic. The artifacts became traits in a scheme of cultural taxonomic units defined by the sharing of traits.

Study of the distribution of such cultural complexes was seen as a preliminary stage in the establishment of chronological relationships. Traits associated with known historic groups provided the links for tracing tribal identity to earlier prehistoric groups represented by trait complexes.

Here the reader should remember (see p. 31) that the artifacts described in chapter VIII are only a part of the archaeological evidence of prehistoric activities. Ephemeral soil stains and such unimposing material as animal bones and charcoal are also part of the archaeological record. Analysis and observations of such evidence is critical for understanding prehistoric activities.

The last topic discussed is prehistoric copper mining and utilization of copper. Hinsdale urged study and preservation of copper mining and technology especially on Isle Royale. Hinsdale visited the copper mines on the Keweenaw peninsula himself in 1925. By the 1920s Isle Royale had attracted various scientific investigators. Scientific investigation of the island by the University of Michigan Museum of Anthropology, Museum of Zoology, Herbarium, Department of Geography and Department of Geology was funded by a state appropriation in 1929. Fred Dustin was employed in 1929 by the Museum of Anthropology to survey archaeological sites on Isle Royale. The Museum expedition to the island was conducted under the direction of Carl Guthe in 1930. An act of Congress in 1931 authorized the establishment of Isle Royale as a national park. The park was formally dedicated in 1946 (Haight 1946). No doubt the preservation of the prehistoric remains of Isle Royale within a national park pleased Hinsdale.

CONCLUSIONS

In conclusion, Hinsdale's interests were not narrowly focused on a simple inventory of archaeological sites or even archaeological problems alone, but extended to broader anthropological topics. Perhaps his greatest contribution is that he placed Michigan prehistory in a broad anthropological context. Hinsdale's contribution to the study of Michigan archaeology include: (1) efforts toward preservation of Michigan prehistory, (2) participation in the founding of a state archaeological society, (3) beginning of an ecological approach to prehistory in Michigan, (4) compilation of existing data that remains a useful reference even today.

The most important message of the book is that the prehistory of Michigan is worthy of study and preservation. Further, the general public may not only contribute to the study and preservation of cultural resources but their participation is essential. An aware and knowledgeable public is necessary for the protection of cultural resources. A general appreciation and sensitivity to the significance of cultural resources will help to reduce destruction of cultural resources through simple curiosity, accidental exposure and thoughtless looting for selfish gain. Further, public support is needed for legislation and funding to preserve and study prehistory. People who wish to participate more actively as avocational archaeologists may join the Michigan Archaeological Society and attend its functions and receive its publications.

Today, even more so than in the 1920s, destruction because of road and urban construction, borrow pits and erosion continues. Since soil disturbance is proceeding at such a rapid rate it is impossible for professionals to monitor and react to all such activity. Therefore, avocational archaeologists and the interested public must be relied on for cooperation to reduce impending destruction and to mitigate accidental exposure of sites.[1]

[1]The author wishes to thank H. Wright, P. Welch and M. Shott for reading and commenting on earlier drafts of this introduction.

INTRODUCTION

The motive in preparing an introduction to Michigan archaeology is to bring to public attention, as forcefully as possible, the fact that the state had, and now has, some rather distinctive antiquities. In the interest of education and science, these deserve to be studied, preserved as far as possible, and classified.

The Museum of the University of Michigan would appear to be a proper center from which surveys may be directed, at least until a better and permanent arrangement can be made. The desire is to cooperate with every society, organization, and individual interest that is disposed to lend its influence to the same effort.

The old haphazard method of digging here and collecting there, with only the assembling of a collection in view, cannot lead to any useful results. The state should be plotted and worked in sections. Perhaps the county would be a convenient unit for study, but counties are purely artificial districts. A more rational and scientific division would be the natural regions, such as the River Raisin Valley, the Saginaw Basin, the Grand River Drainage Area, etc. Collaborators could investigate their local and adjoining units in such a way that when sufficient facts and data are assembled, an archaeological atlas, by counties or districts, might be issued as a state document or bulletin.

Such a conception can amount to little unless the state does two things: First, takes steps to preserve the remaining works from further damage and destruction;

and, second, authorizes some society, department, or staff to direct the exploration and at the same time advise individual investigators regarding methods of work and the collection and collation of data. A comprehensive plan contemplating several years in its development should be adopted. A permanent center for activity should be established. Nearly every state, except Michigan, has some machinery through which its antiquities are being studied. Ohio publishes, annually, a report upon field work done under its authorization and by its financial aid. Its State Archaeological Society has issued as a state publication a magnificent atlas containing reports and maps of every county. Wisconsin, for over twenty years, has been doing the same kind of archaeological research and publishes a monthly magazine upon the subject. New York, also, maintains a staff of archaeological experts and from time to time issues excellent reports. The provinces of Canada are doing field work similar to that of the foremost of our states.

States, working as units in their respective fields, are able to furnish to the American Bureau of Ethnology material for use in compiling its voluminous reports. One looks with little satisfaction through government publications, such as the Smithsonian Reports, or Reports of the National Museum, for information concerning Michigan. Some articles about Michigan were published in a few old volumes, none in recent years.

Several states have bought and preserved as state parks, lands upon which important remains are standing, so that they may become of lasting value to those who care to study them. The legislature of Illinois has just appropriated $50,000 for the purchase of the site of the Cahokia group of mounds at East St. Louis.

Whoever takes the time to read these pages will be impressed with the meagerness and the vagueness of the data presented. The latter are the siftings from many records, reports, papers, letters, and conversations upon the subject. The very desultory nature of what is presented should stimulate readers to the determination, even at this late day, to replace conjecture with accurate information, and unsystematized spasmodic effort with organized surveys.

In the first chapter, which deals with the question of how the American Continent became populated, an effort is made to give some of the conflicting views that are held by ethnologists, geologists and geographers, and to portray something of the Indian racial traits and grades of culture. It is a far-away approach to the local problem, but may give a somewhat useful background.

Since it is explained in the first chapter how man might have come to America, some other rather conjectural matter is presented in the second chapter upon his behavior in the Michigan peninsulas. The third chapter is an attempt to define briefly, and explain, some of the common terms used in the study of man as a social creature. The fourth chapter, upon Indian relic collecting, attempts to show what is valuable and what is worthless in collections and how they should be catalogued. The other chapters, under different captions, roughly outline the material or physical properties of early man in Michigan.

No one knows better than the writer the immature nature of his efforts, but he puts forth, as partial excuse, the fact that the subject matter itself is in an undeveloped stage. Like the world stuff, in the scriptural outline of creation: It is "without form, and void."

Archaeology practically closes where written records begin. It undertakes to determine what happened among men before they were capable of preparing tabulated accounts of themselves or when such accounts as they have left have to be interpreted by means of keys and comparative philology.

The characteristics of the peoples living in the state at the time of, and since, the white settlers and their fore-runners, the Catholic missionaries, are well portrayed in descriptions to be found in the voluminous Jesuit Rela-tions, in reports of officers serving under different gov-ernments which have held sway here, and in accounts of venturesome travelers.

There seemed to be a tendency all over the world, the American continents included, towards slowly shifting migrations, so that in a few centuries there was consider-able change in positions of tribes. Archaeology can help to trace those shiftings. It is the only means we have of ascertaining whether the historic groups were the original proprietors of the land or whether they were intrusive upon a former population.

No attempt is made to locate or trace the migrations of any of the Michigan tribes, except so far as references to them are used for illustrating other points. However, there are living in Michigan at this time over five thou-sand Indians who should be studied before their entire ethnological value is gone.

Complete as restorations may be of the lost and dis-appearing monumental remains of a vanished race, with all artifacts and habiliments of their time collected into museums and written up in books by scientific men, the atmosphere of the Indian's world cannot be restored.   To visualize, so to speak, the atmosphere of the peoples whom he studies, is the ideal of the anthropologist.

Twenty-five years ago, Mr. Harlan I. Smith advocated and pleaded for a survey in Michigan that has not yet been commenced. This review is but a feeble attempt to arouse the same interest for which he worked. Reference must be made to the newly organized Michigan State Archaeological Society. It sets out with the right purpose and a wide vision of the field that lies before it. An impulse received from the society's first meeting led the writer to this compilation.

If it had not been for the assistance of a large number of persons this effort would have entirely failed, but few collectors having been reluctant in loaning specimens for illustrations or furnishing photographs and drawings that could be used for such a purpose. Among those who havè rendered material aid and to whom sincere acknowledgement is made are: Professor R. Clyde Ford, Ypsilanti; Mr. George R. Fox, President of the Michigan State Archaeological Society, Three Oaks; Mr. Edward J. Stevens, Secretary of the Michigan State Archaeological Society, Kalamazoo; Mr. Fred Dustin, Saginaw; Mr. H. L. Ward, Director, Kent Scientific Museum, Grand Rapids; Mr. Donald O. Boudeman, Kalamazoo; Mr. G. X. Allen, Bay City; Mr. William Barr, Saline; Dr. William Durand, Marshall; Mr. G. R. Fuller, Grand Ledge; Mr. Claude Hamilton, Grand Rapids; Mr. B. Knobloch, Detroit; Mr. C. W. Manktelow, Cadillac; Mr. H. C. Moore, Flint; Mr. Charles Morrison, Williamston; Mr. George R. Philp, Lake City; Mr. W. W. Potter, Lansing; Dr. C. S. Purdy, Buckley; Mr. J. T. Reeder, Houghton; Mr. J. B. Richardson, Bay City; Mr. E. H. Sanders, Battle Creek; Mr. J. W. Sanders.

Charlotte; Mr. W. L. Schmidt, Pinconning; Mr. A. L. Sawyer, Menominee; Mr. Jay See, Diamondale; Mr. William I. Boyce, Portland; Mr. R. E. Southwick, Hart; Mr. E. L. Van Wormer, Union City; and members of the staff of the Museum of the University of Michigan.

Like the rest of this volume, the illustrations are meagre. No attempt is made to present more than a few type specimens. Those who look for entertainment from a profusion of cuts will be disappointed.

CHAPTER I

THE PEOPLING OF NORTH AMERICA

ORIGIN OF THE FIRST AMERICANS

Many thousand years before the landings at James-town, Plymouth Rock, in Florida, in Mexico; before Columbus had come to some West Indian island; before Norsemen had touched somewhere from Labrador to Rhode Island; Old World migrants had gained a foot-hold in northwestern North America. This did not occur until men had made considerable progress in mental capacity, possessed themselves of many material proper-ties, and had developed some social progress, but it was a very recent event in the history of mankind.

Possible Routes of Travel. It is generally main-tained that the route of migration was across the places where the channels of open water or of ice were quite narrow; that is, at Bering Strait, or from island to island in the immediate vicinity. As to the time when the first crossing that resulted in permanent settlement was made, there is some disagreement. There is also disagreement in opinion as to whether the original immigrants came in considerable numbers for a short period, migration then ceasing; or whether it continued at intervals for a long period.

There appears to be a marked similarity between the American Indians and some of the northeastern Asiatic tribes. In racial features color has significance, so much so that we refer to the white, the black, and the yellow

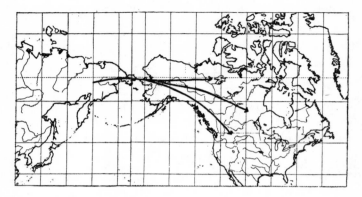

DIAGRAM ILLUSTRATING POSSIBLE MIGRATION ROUTES INTO
NORTH AMERICA

races. The shade of the skin is by no means so important in classification as hairiness of the body and anatomical features, especially those of the cranium. The character of the teeth sheds light upon racial classification. The shovel-shaped incisor is found in over ninety per cent. of pure Indians. It is a pronounced peculiarity of the Asiatic Mongoloids and rare among Europeans and Negroes. Before somatologists commit themselves definitely, however, very much remains to be found out concerning Mongoloids.

The possibility of wayfarers from Asia arriving upon the western shores by way of some of the islands in the broad Pacific has received serious consideration. There are those who maintain that the ancient Mexican and South American cultures show evidences of Chinese, Polynesian, and even of Egyptian intrusions. This will be referred to later. The majority of Americanists do not appear to accept such a supposition as probable. However, owing to the fact that the evidence in the

American question is not all in, judgment appears to be more or less in suspension and controversy goes on.

No Contact with Advanced Civilizations Evident. If there was at any time contact with an advanced civilization of the Old World, the proof is meager if not entirely lacking. Such contacts, it seems, if at all frequent, would have brought to the aborigines seeds of useful plants, animals and fowls of domestication, principles of building lodges with chimneys, sails and oar-locks, the wheel, the smelting of metals, and social customs that could be recognized without forced analogies.

Primitive Traits Possessed in Common

The presumption is that some savage bands of Asiatics, among the first to become Americans, were accompanied by dogs. The dog was the only really domesticated beast common to the two continents until the Spaniards, in historic times, introduced the horse. The Esquimaux probably had lines of communication with Siberia, where they could have obtained some useful notions they did not have previously.

Resemblances in Stone Work. There have been found striking resemblances in a few forms of stone work, such as gouges, hatchet heads, worked nuggets of metal, slim slate spears, etc., suggestive of diffusion from the western side of the Eastern Continent. Such slate spears are found in Michigan. These coincidences have not been generally accepted as convincing proof of a common origin and are not outside the neolithic phase. There are English scholars, however, who see Mediterranean influences in American antiquities. If any antique specimens turn out to have a central origin they do not bear upon the question of trans-oceanic influence within the Iron Age.

Pre-migration Traits of the Stone Age Man. It has been possible to make a rather accurate estimate of the traits, habits, and skill that had been acquired before the Stone Age man came from his Old World habitat. Among the equipment which he brought with him may be mentioned: methods of making fire, stone-flaking, and chipping; the throwing-stick which lengthens the reach of the arm, thereby accelerating the velocity of the projectile and serving the function of the bow; the harpoon; the capacity for simple basket and net making; the boiling of food by putting hot stones into vessels of water; and, necessarily, the making of such vessels. He decorated his body with pigments and may have made the pigments permanent by tattooing. The use of string, twines, and cordage is fundamental; without these there could be no human progress. The Stone Age man was infested with parasites; so were the dogs that came with him. Pediculids and fleas are cosmopolitan and known to be of great antiquity. He knew how to hunt, fish, dig edible foods from shore, field, and forest; and collected wild berries and fruits. Imagination filled his world with mysterious powers which could manifest themselves in living and in inanimate objects and give them an inward life. He lived in an imaginary as well as a real environment. A kind of specialized 'go-between,' priest, or shaman, negotiated for him with the powers. He set apart or recognized certain places as especially facilitating religious and magical doings. Shrines and temples were later conceptions. He must have built shelters for himself, but the chimney was never used in any of his structures.

Neolithic Inventions Filtered into America. Cultural elements and mechanical contrivances occasionally filtered into America after population became fixed and considerably disseminated. If the first settlers came in late paleolithic times, they must have walked over upon the ice, because boats and rafts are thought not to have been invented until the neolithic period. The bow and arrow, considered so distinctive of the Indian's armamentarium, is also a neolithic invention, but came early into his possession if he did not bring it with him. The boat or canoe became distributed throughout both Americas wherever water communication was possible.

The built-up, composite, 'sinew-backed,' bow found its way from Asia into northwestern America two or three thousand years ago. Tailored clothing, a kind of armor made of wooden slats, conical skin tents, and dog traction, are examples of intrusions at various early times. With all allowances for dissemination and borrowing from the Old World, enough of the Indian outfitting sprang originally from local necessities to make American culture characteristically distinctive.

Various Views as to the Origins of Culture Divergencies

G. Elliot Smith, in expressing his views upon the dissemination of culture contents, states that the elements of the ancient civilizations of India, farther Asia, Malay Archipelago, Oceania, and America, were brought in succession to each of these places by mariners whose trading intercourse began between the Mediterranean and India sometime after 800 B.C.; that they played upon the Pacific littoral of America and introduced the germs of pre-Columbian civilization. This theory would be strengthened if a few recognizable 'foreign' words from these Mediterranean mariners had been incorporated into the native American language. The majority of anthropologists do not agree with Smith's extreme views, but they are presented here so that the reader, if not familiar with the subject, may know that there are different opinions as to the origins of American culture.

Views of the 'Diffusion' School. The line is sharply drawn between the two schools of anthropologists. The one adheres strictly to the idea of diffusion and does not accept the theory that independent inventions of the same things were made at various places and at various times. They would not accede to MacCulloch's[1] statement: "Similar conditions of life, similar environments, similar stages of culture, similar mental and psychic states will almost invariably work out mental, artistic, and mechanical products in precisely the same way."

The 'Parallelism' Idea. The other school accepts parallelism and maintains that American culture is largely autochthonous. Some sort of flood myth was told nearly the world over. The Indians had versions of it. Blood sacrifice in some form or other was widely practised. The legend of the magic flight extended from Scandinavia, where it probably did not originate, through Europe, into Africa, to the Pacific Islands, across Asia, and patterns of it appear in American mythology. Boas thinks probably such myths as the magic flight and the flood may have come to America after the discovery, from Portugal, Spain, and through the medium of the Negroes. That being so, these myths do not have a historical connection with the pre-Columbian lore. They were abruptly injected into it. The French and Scotch also grafted stories into the lore of the Canadian Indians. These modern introductions are said to be

[1] The Childhood of Fiction, p. 471.

sharply distinguishable from the native folk-tales. According to the Oregon and British Columbia version of the race between the turtle and the rabbit, the turtle won by a shrewd trick and not by persistence. Turtle places his brothers, who look just like him, along the various points of the race course and in this way makes Rabbit believe he has won. The channel through which this fable reached the place in which it was current lacks spatial continuity because it was not known along the lines that it should have traveled. How did it 'jump' from either Asiatic or European sources? Around the Great Lakes, the deluge story is: that a new earth was created by diving animals who saved themselves on a raft from which one after another dived until Muskrat brought up some mud from which was created a new world; quite a different narrative from the scriptural story of the Noahcian deluge.

Mexican Accomplishments. The Mexicans were astronomers and mathematicians. They used a series of animal signs similar to the zodiac and made use of the zero in arithmetic before the Hindus, to whom is generally assigned its origin. This being true, those who hold to diffusion as against the possibility of independent origins will have to explain how a Yucatan concept reached Egypt and Western Asia by an adverse turning of the current.

The Maya of Central America had symbols for days, months, years, and cycles. They recorded dates upon native papyrus and carved them with stone gravers upon monuments, or molded them in adobe. These inscriptions attest two important facts: first, the central Americans had invented a kind of glyptic writing; and second, they had a very accurate knowledge of the periodic

occurrences of celestial phenomena. In these things
Smith sees the influence of traders bearing Egyptian
culture across Asia and the Pacific Ocean. If, by the
time of Christ, groups of Americans springing from
savage Mongoloids had progressed thus far toward a
civilization, the evidence is somewhat convincing that the
occupancy of the continent covered a period of several
thousand years.

Borrowing versus Originality. As stated previously,
a spirited discussion, which amounts to a controversy,
goes on between those who believe that very many tools,
folkways, and myths have been separate and independent inventions in different parts of the world, and those
who hold the contrary opinion. The latter say the only
rational view is that inventions have been made but once
and then dispersed to the places where they occur. According to this idea borrowing was a fundamental process in human progress. We are likely to take for granted
that when man came to a certain point of differentiation
from brute, devices and beliefs were spontaneous products of his mental processes. Because an idea seems
simple, and a tale or myth childlike to us, we regard
them as easy and even natural results of the activity of
the primitive mind. If that be so, the 'primitive' mind
is not primitive. Many examples of continuous distribution are found connecting Old World traits with those
of the New. Sporadic resemblances are not lacking, but
resemblances must be analyzed before being accepted as
identical. The Indians made inventions similar to those
found in the same grade of culture elsewhere, and also
developed new complexes, but the idea of originality
must be regarded with caution and each case examined
separately, with the presumption in favor of dissemination.

The extreme view, that inventions rarely, if ever, occur independently, as held by G. Elliot Smith and his 'School,' having been stated, the following from Professor Ogburn[2] is a statement of the other view which is widely held: "There is a good deal of evidence to indicate that the accumulation or growth of culture reaches a stage where certain inventions, if not inevitable, are certainly to a high degree probable, given a certain level of mentality. The fact that an invention is independently made in several localities suggests such a cultural preparation. This probability of an invention due to cultural preparations is more noticeable perhaps in later cultures than in earlier cultures."

Lowie[3] states the opinion held by the greater number of American anthropologists in these words: "Yet in this country this notion of diffusion has not been carried to extremes; while a very large portion of any particular culture may be admitted to come from an alien home, it is generally recognized that occasionally, even though rarely, a new idea arises spontaneously and that such lucky chance may be repeated."

Simple Inventions more likely to be Independent. As regards independent invention the argument is something like this: Is it simpler or more or less complex? We may think of a piece of string used for binding and tying as simple, but when it becomes warp and woof of a fabric the product is complex. A single strand was more apt to be put to simple uses in many places than that the weaving of cloth was likely to have been invented several times.

A story with but one actor and one act is more likely to come into many heads than is a plot or yarn with

2 Social Change, p. 343.
3 American Mercury, April, 1924.

varied motifs. Inventions came slowly to early man. It was thousands of years in the paleolithic period after he had flaked flint on one side (Aurignacian) before he flaked it upon both sides (Solutrian). It was 50,000 years from the time he used worked stones for pounding and cutting until he attached handles to them. Iron did not come into use until three or four thousand years ago and its distribution was very gradual. There is a kind of parallelism between invention in culture, and mutation in biology. Both are sports from prevailing types. One pattern of explanation will not cover all cultures because cultures are not uniform.

Were the Primitive Americans a Homogeneous People?

Dixon's Methods of Analysis. It is admitted upon all sides that the racial history of the New World presents a very perplexing ethnological problem. The question largely revolves about the point: Were the primitive Americans a homogeneous people? Dixon, in his methods of analysis, sets out to establish the thesis that they were mixed and not to be classified as even a comparatively uniform group; and that the variations in type cannot be accounted for by the changes which took place after a single period of migration. Everyone recognizes differences in the physical structure of the Indians of different districts. A majority of the investigators ascribe this to variations which occurred in rather isolated communities and then became extended by inter-breeding in a few thousand years.

Dixon's methods of analysis consist mostly of schemes of skull measurements, cephalic index, length-height index, and nasal index, which, when applied to peoples of

northeastern Asia, whence came the Americans, prove
them to be of varying racial composition. He states that
the necessities of the situation force the conclusion: that
there must have been not one wave of longer or shorter
duration of immigrants, but many waves at different
times, each being a variant in type, just as the population from which they came and of which they were a
part at the time of leaving had varied, mostly by admix-
tures, from their predecessors. In applying his threefold
tests to American skulls he makes out marginal forms
unlike central forms. He deduces that certain heads,
being marginal, and according to biological formula,
older, were of a much earlier period than the heads of
the central Algonquians, for instance. According to
Dixon and some other scholars, the Indians are descen-
dants of mixed strains of ancestry. While there is no
American race, as previously stated, a number of those
who work upon the problem maintain that the Indians
were in all probability descended from an original and
quite uniform group of Mongoloids.

When Migrations Began. There has been disagreement of opinion among ethnologists as to when migrations began. Some hold that the western continents were
not inhabited until a considerable time after the last
glaciation; others, that there are unmistakable evidences
of the presence of man before then. There seems, at
present, to be a disposition to fix the advent of man upon
this side of the Pacific soon after the retreat of the last
ice sheet, or about eight or ten thousand years ago; however, such opinion is strongly contested. It is anticipated
that evidence will be found which will be convincing to
all scientific men as to the time and the people of the
first settlements in America. Meantime one may have

an open mind, awaiting the conclusion. Professor Harris
H. Wilder[4] gives an excellent discussion of the prehistory of the two Americas. After presenting the evidence
for and against remote migration he states: ''The more
conservative view, however, still is, that the Indian was
a comparatively late arrival, that he found the continent
at the time of his advent entirely unoccupied by human
beings, and that we have as yet no absolutely definite
records of any previous race who may have occupied a
portion of it at an earlier time.''

Migration is not often of free volition. Movements
are matters of welfare. There must be pressure to drive
men from an old and familiar environment into a new
one. If the group is to exist in a place into which it is
pushed, conditions of subsistence must be tolerable. Until men arrived where they did not fear conflict with, and
oppression from, their own species, the urge was from
the rear of the flank. Once across the straits there was,
at first, no human hindrance to territorial expansion.
There was freedom to go wherever there were no natural
obstructions to the pathway. Savages are lacking in the
explorer's ambition and curiosity. They drift in lines
of easiest movement. A time came, finally, after the
immigrants had increased in numbers, partly by the
addition of later arrivals, when the old causes became
operative and pressure accelerated travel toward the
south or along the Arctic coast. Gradual changes in
location tended toward adaptations and the fixing of
variations in type.

It is admitted that there were narrow-headed, medium-
headed, and broad-headed Indians. Kroeber, Wissler,
Hrdlička, Holmes, Boas and many others, maintain that

[4] Man's Prehistoric Past, p. 295.

from the point of view of race classification, the cephalic index does not yield broad enough results. Boas makes a rather severe criticism of Dixon's methods of analysis.

Language Problem a Confusing One. The languages of the two Americas are a tangled skein. According to Powell's classification, which has not been much modified, there are perhaps more language stocks here than in all the rest of the world. Attempts have been made to use the language groups in some kind of interpretation of origins, but they are very confusing, except to specialists who themselves disagree. Wissler[5] says: "So far, no evidence has come to hand that would identify a single New World language with an Old World stock."

GENERAL SOCIAL CONDITIONS OF THE AMERICAN INDIAN

Real Property Communal. The Indian's conception of property was the communal system. Individuals had no real estate. The lands were common property of the tribe. Privileges of hunting were accorded to groups. Each tribe defended its own hunting grounds against intruders. To the women belonged the house and a few personal items of domestic use. The man owned his hunting and war equipment. Barter was common, but exchanges were never made with the idea of profit. The Indian did not have our conception of values nor of buying and selling. Profit and loss did not enter into his reckoning.

The Mexicans and the Incas elaborated the communal system more thoroughly than has ever been done by any other people. There were yearly allotments of land to households for tillage. Their land laws and codes were very exacting.

[5] The American Indian, p. 396.

Maintenance Complex Dominant.   The Indian's routine of life was much like our own, a continual effort to maintain existence.   His food was mixed, but more mixed in some regions than in others.   Where edible vegetables and seeds grew naturally, or could be cultivated, they entered into his dietary.   But owing to climatic conditions, the Esquimo was largely carnivorous. The hunting tribes that followed the caribou and buffalo also subsisted largely upon flesh.   Those who lived along shores and streams obtained a large supply of food from the water.   A strip of the northwest coast is known as the 'salmon area.'   Many tribes of the California area ate largely of wild seeds, mostly acorns, which they ground into meal and cooked.   Agriculture prevailed extensively east of the Mississippi and south of the St. Lawrence to the Atlantic.   The intensive agricultural district was Mexico, Central America, and a strip of South America west of the Andes.   'Casava,' or manioc the root from which tapioca is obtained, was cultivated extensively in eastern South America.   Elsewhere, throughout the large agricultural area, Indian corn was the staple.   Corn is the substantial native cereal of America and the process from planting to mush is quite complex, and different from the complexes of other seeds. The planting was different; so was the care of the growing plant.   If the growth was not arrested for eating in the green stage, corn had to be harvested, stored, shelled, milled, and cooked.   Every corn-crib is a monument to the Indians' contribution of one of the world's greatest staples.   The aroma from pipes wherever smoked throughout the world is an incense to the American who discovered the 'divine weed.'   Beans and squashes were generally cultivated in the corn or maize area.   In the making of sugar from the sap of maple trees an interesting complex of inventions was involved, showing much originality. There was scarifying of the trees, the sap spout, the sap bucket, the boiling pot, the firing process, and the final moulding of the semi-fluid product of evaporation in the mocucks.

The Mexicans, besides using the corn which they developed from some native grass, raised potatoes, sweet potatoes, peppers, and other indigenous vegetables. Vegetable oils were extracted from seeds, hickory and other nuts. Artichokes grew wild over a wide territory and were also cultivated. If all the plants that were cultivated by the natives before 1492 were listed, there would be more than forty of them. Wild rice was depended upon to help out the food supply throughout the western part of the Great Lakes Region. Jenks, as a result of a very careful study, estimates that, owing to the easy procurement of wild rice, a strip about seventy-five miles wide and one hundred and fifty to two hundred miles long, comprising the small lake territory of Wisconsin, sustained a population greater than all the rest of Wisconsin, Minnesota, Illinois, Indiana, Michigan, and Ohio combined. The seed of the wild rice was sowed in the water by some of the tribes. One or two of the tribes had a taboo against sowing wild rice, but did not hesitate to forage upon the territories of others, which gives an economic explanation of the warfare that frequently prevailed among the Chippewas, Menominees, Dakotas, and Winnebagoes. There was a war in the vicinity of Green Bay between the Chippewas and the Menominees known as the Sturgeon War. The name very clearly describes the economic issue. Agriculture made it possible for a larger population to subsist in a given area and conduced to stabilization.

Wherever vegetable foods were used, some kind of dinner pot was necessary. The distribution of pottery corresponds roughly to the agricultural areas.

The Mexicans and South Americans cultivated cotton which they spun into yarns and wove into textiles. The fibers of several wild plants were also spun and woven in many places. The fleeces and hairy coats of some animals were used for the making of woolens.

Population. The population of the Americas was never very great. At the time of the coming of the white men the total number of Indians, north of Mexico, was not far from 1,150,000. That was about the limit of the load the territory could carry under the conditions of obtaining subsistence. The saturation point appears to have been reached.

Earth Monuments and Public Houses. The Indians built monuments, usually in the form of mounds of earth, to their dead. These they dedicated with religious ceremony and sometimes maintained as shrines. Many of them built what would be called in New England town houses. These houses were dedicated to worship and to secular councils. Those who account for every similarity of occurrence, of course, cannot admit that the Iroquois 'long-house' was original with the builders. Council fires have burned and council lodges have been built nearly the world over. They seem to be a production of a certain level of social development; or to be consistent with the diffusion doctrine, to have been disseminated or borrowed from one single original but very ancient source, from which they traveled around the globe. In their architecture and carvings, the Mexicans and some of the South Americans equalled, if they did not surpass, any other Stone Age men. Their temples and public buildings of massive ashlars are the world's wonder.

When they were first disturbed by the incoming of white men, the natives were in the recent stone age of culture, although in the central belt the making of bronze ceremonials and trinkets was going on. If they had not been disturbed, a more or less civilized status might have been evolved. Be that as it may, it is too late now. The native American has become a museum specimen, a ward of a tribe of later immigrants.

CHAPTER II

GEOGRAPHICAL AND OTHER PECULIARITIES OF MICHIGAN

Semi-insular Location of the State. Michigan lies almost in the center of a continent, but its situation is somewhat remarkable when considered with reference to the Indians' mode of travel. The state is almost insular. The Lower Peninsula is cut off from land approach upon all sides except the south. The Upper Peninsula also projects into a wide expanse of water and can be entered by land only from one direction, the west. The straits between the two parts of the state permitted crossings by canoes and rafts, but he would have been a bold adventurer who attempted to cross Lakes Superior, Michigan, or Huron in any craft known to the Indians. However, Schoolcraft believes that bold and experienced canoemen found no difficulty in crossing Lake Michigan from shore to shore in calm summer months. Coming into the country necessitated following the shores or seeking the narrow places. The Southern Peninsula was readily accessible by dug-outs and canoes at Mackinaw and the St. Clair and Detroit rivers, but there was no free sweep of open country from all directions as in the case of all the other states except Florida.

In early historic times different tribes, pursued by others, were fleeing from lower Michigan. The escape was along the shores of the lakes at the north or by land towards the south. The distance from one of these outlets to the other is over three hundred miles. A frag-

ment of the Hurons, known as Wyandottes, who after-
ward had to be reckoned with in northern and western
Ohio, came into Michigan from Canada around the head
of Lake Huron. Those fearful warriors, the Iroquois,
from the St. Lawrence and New York regions, drove the
Hurons along the shore-line; neither the pursuers nor
the pursued ventured across the wide part of the lake.

Crossings were made at the rivers that flow into and
out of Lake St. Clair, and there was the entrance by land
from the Ohio country.   Judge C. I. Walker[6] says: ''The
region around Detroit was not favorable residence
ground for the tribes because it was on the war path of
the Iroquois who carried their terrors as far west as the
Illinois Country.'' These facts are mentioned to illus-
trate, in this connection, what has been referred to as
the rather isolated situation of the state in regard to
primitive means of travel. It may have had its influence
in retarding and circumscribing migration, but the iso-
lation was not complete enough to develop a distinctive
type of culture, as occurred in Mexico, unless the 'formal' garden beds be regarded as locally distinctive.

Who were the first immigrants into this inter-lake
country? There are but slight clues as to how many
waves of people came and went. Were the tribes living
here at the time of the advent of the white man the original 'proprietors' of the soil? Some are known to have
been transient; of others one cannot speak so positively.
It is impossible to build up much of a theory upon the
available data. One thing is certain, the first comers
were reacting to the same influences that had led to the
populating of the continent thousands of years before.
There is a similarity between the land situation of our

[6] Michigan Pioneer Collections, Vol. VIII, p. 419.

peninsulas and that of the continent.   Both are bordered
by wide waters, but the peninsulas not completely so.

Study by Stratification in Michigan not Fruitful.
Some of the methods of determining different periods of
occupation cannot be used here because the conditions
of their application do not exist, but they deserve mention as a part of the general subject.   For example,
study by superposition or stratification we can use but
feebly, if at all.   In caves and rock shelters that have
been human habitations, the lower layers of accumulated
dirt, ashes, and refuse show, sometimes, forms of implements, patterns of pottery, and bones of animals, different from the layers above.   Sometimes several strata are
found, each revealing that people of markedly different
habits and customs had lived there at different times.
The lowest stratum would, of course, represent the first
and oldest dwellers.   The top layer would be witness of
the modes of life, kinds of tools and utensils, and of foods
of the last residents in that place.   Sometimes the debris
of caves is uniform, attesting that but one kind of domestic culture had prevailed throughout the period of habitation.   By measuring the thickness of the layers and
comparing them, one with the other, the relative duration of each period of inhabitance can be determined.
Since Michigan has very few caves and places that would
serve as natural home-shelters, this method of superposition is of but slight use; however, Bela Hubbard's[7]
description of the large mounds upon the first terrace of
Grand River, below Grand Rapids, suggests a degree of
stratification.

Middens.   In many places, California, Florida, Long
Island, and the Maine Coast, large shell heaps are found
along the shores of the ocean and the banks of rivers.

[7] Memorials of a Half-Century, p. 112.

There are extensive river shell heaps in Tennessee. These shells have been piled up as the leavings of the people who ate the clams, oysters, and other mollusks they contained. Some of the shell piles, usually called middens, cover hundreds of square rods of surface and are several feet deep. If, in the bottom layer of such a pile, mixed with the shells, ashes, and pieces of charred wood, roughly flaked stone implements only are found; and, if towards the top, layers should yield pieces of pottery, bones of deer, and well-made tools, the evidence, as to a difference between those who had gathered and eaten shell-fish there at different times and thrown the shells upon the refuse heap of kitchen garbage, is as conclusive as if the fact had been written in a field book when the people were present. Mr. Harlan I. Smith reports three such shell heaps in Michigan, but the state does not afford much opportunity for study of this kind.

Mounds have been investigated with reference to stratification in Wisconsin, Ohio, New York, and many other states, because some of them, when excavated, show they were built up with different layers at different times. Where mounds are, as is generally the case of those in Michigan, simple piles of earth or sand thrown up, probably in a short time, they afford no opportunities for study by superposition. There are stratified mounds on Kratz Creek, Wisconsin. One group showed, from the stratification, at least two cultures, by differences of construction and contents. Each was quite distinct from the other. Probably people of one culture had laid the foundation and perhaps, for their purposes, finished the construction. Another group came on to the ground later and superimposed their own upon the original work as a foundation. They built with different kinds of material and left imbedded therein some specimens of their own tools and wares as well as the bones of their dead.

Nearly all mounds were, undoubtedly, a part of the burial customs of their builders, since a large majority of them contain human remains. In Ohio, there are mounds whose contents are so different, one from another, that two and perhaps three types of culture can be made out. A study of the Indian remains of New York has led to a similar conclusion. In the southwest, perhaps more has been learned from the strata in caves and shelters than elsewhere in this country. Mammoth Cave, Kentucky, seems also to have been occupied by different groups, at least the refuse heaps in the cave seem to be pretty clearly stratified. It is in the Old World, particularly in Europe, where superposition is of so great value in making out classifications in quite minute detail.

Michigan not a Barren Archaeological Field. Michigan has been generally considered as rather barren archaeological ground. She has no striking monumental works; however, no systematic survey of the state has been undertaken and students have found more inviting opportunity elsewhere or in other subjects. It is almost too late, because a very large number of structures have been destroyed or mutilated by untrained relic hunters whose findings are mostly lost or scattered. Those finds that remain in the hands of different persons are apt to be lacking in data that should render them of educational and scientific value. A too pessimistic attitude should not be assumed, though one cannot help feeling regret for loss and carelessness. Many very interesting and instructive mounds have been used as supplies for road-building materials, others have been plowed down by farmers in their agricultural pursuits, and still others have given way to buildings and to factories, as occurred in the cities of Detroit, Port Huron, and Grand Rapids. Counts of various structures and land marks both extant and destroyed, presented elsewhere in this volume, indicate that the archaeological values of Michigan have been underestimated.

Michigan must have been a rather inviting territory in which to hunt, fish, and gather wild rice. Agriculture, after the Indians' fashion, was carried on, and maple sugar was made in the hardwood belt. The hundreds of lakes and rivers made inland travel convenient. The bark canoe center was the lake region. The state is upon the fringe of the mound building area that centered along the Ohio River. It may be a question whether it was a land of long, permanent residence of any groups of people or whether tribes came and went more or less at random according to their needs and strength. Some tribes were probably quite restive, others more sedentary, especially those of the Lower Peninsula which engaged in agriculture. Mixing of the loosely organized groups was going on all the time. Prisoners became adopted sons, women were stolen and became mothers in other tribes, federations were made and members of weak communities were assimilated by the stronger, so that stocks were not much more than theoretically akin.

Determining Factors of Culture. Aside from the physical features of a territory, the nature of the plant and animal life is a part of the determining factors of the culture type. Peoples living in open plains and grassy prairies would have different adaptations from those living in a forested district. A plains' Indian would have little use for a birch bark canoe and not much more for wood-working tools. A forest dweller would not have many implements made from buffalo bones.

CHAPTER III

DEFINITIONS

Elementary and discursive as these pages may be a term or two will have to be used that may need defining.

Culture.—The word culture has a technical as well as a popular meaning. Everyone is a part of and lives in a culture, although, in the common use of the word, he may not be cultured. In the latter sense, culture means refinement of manners, polish, and conformity to the conventionalities of society. We refer to learned people as being cultured. There is a culture in the use of language. One may be cultured in music or history.

In the intimate view of mankind, culture means modes of life. "It is the sum total of all the activities of a community." We live in our culture, which is continuous although individuals are constantly dropping out. Savages live in their culture. There are no human beings so near the borderline of the brute as to be without culture. All mankind has modes of living. They have motives and habits of thought. They produce and consume. They have family and neighborhood relations. Everything that pertains to existence in and among a group of persons is a part of their culture. The thousands of things that appertain to the culture in which we live, dwellings, tools, machinery, domestic animals, politics, religion, schools, automobiles, telephones, newspapers, postal service, voting and holding office, manners, dress, securing and preparing foods, and whatever else we live by, in, and with, constitute our culture. So far as different communities have different manners, use different things and think different thoughts, their cultures vary from one another. The culture of a Chippewa Indian was made up in part of his bark house, canoe, bow, arrows and spear, pottery, stone axes and other tools, clothing, methods of securing game, fish, and other foods, moccasins and so on. He danced, sang, gambled, worshipped, fought, had a family, raised corn, beans, and tobacco, cooperated with his fellows, all of which, together with everything else with which he had to do and with which he lived, including what he thought, constituted his culture. The Indian's habits of thought were as distinctive as his physical properties. His mind was in the pre-analytical stage. He was intensely emotional and a mystic in religion. He was ardent in his beliefs and the true relations between cause and effect did not always enter into his deductions. He gave great heed to ritual and magic. He believed there were indwelling spirits in whatever appeared to be outside the common or the ordinary. In his religion, he manifested slight distinctions between right or wrong, good or bad. His religion, when manifested through acts, was mostly propitiatory.

That part of culture that appertains to things is called material culture. Mental culture deals with thoughts, beliefs, and conduct, as its subject matter, and fringes upon and overlaps psychology. Culture as a whole has physical and spiritual manifestations.

By cultural variations and complexes one group of people is distinguished from another. If their cultures were identical, an old-fashioned New England Yankee could not have been distinguished from a Pennsylvania

'Dutchman.' There is a tendency to give the word 'civilization' a distinctive meaning somewhat synonymous with culture. We used to call only those nations civilized that represented the top layer of human refinement in thought and behavior, but now anthropologists speak of the Esquimoian and Patagonian civilizations just as Gibbon referred to the Greek and Roman civilizations and as we refer to the French and English as civilized.

Culture areas.—It would take more than the presence or absence of bird-stones or fluted axes to mark a great variation in a culture area, but they do represent culture variations, and when variations are strikingly numerous and different a culture area may be mapped out. There is quite an agreement in recognizing nine or ten culture areas of North America. The most northern is the Arctic or Esquimo Area. A wide strip of country east of the Rocky Mountains is the Plains Area. Michigan is in the Northeastern Woodland Area. There can be numbers of sub-areas. A sub-area could be made based upon the extensive use of birch bark, or the occurrence of buffalo. There are culture levels. While culture areas differ much according to the means of living that nature enforces upon man, they may be upon about the same level from the standpoint and limitations of accomplishment. Potawatomi and Delawares had variations of culture, but were upon the same culture level. Indians of the woodland area made baskets of splints; the basket makers of the Pacific Coast used fine strands of fiber and employed a different process: two differences in culture as far as the basket arts are concerned. The Michigan Indians used grooved axes; the Iroquois of New York and Canada did not groove their axes. They also differed in their pottery patterns and the way in which they worked the flint into arrow points; hence we say that they had differences in culture, but the differences were comparatively slight.

When differences are cumulative and distinctly striking, one notes a new culture area, as has been explained. There were almost enough culture differences between the Saginaw Valley and the Upper Peninsula regions to make separate areas of them. The denizens of the Saginaw Valley chipped chert nodules into artifacts, they built small mounds, made maple sugar, and practised agriculture. The distinctive trait of the inhabitants of the Lake Superior Region was copper mining and their subsistence was upon flesh and fish more than where food plants could be better cultivated.

Artifact.—The word artifact, used so frequently by archaeologists, signifies something made by hand, especially by the hand of stone age man. Arrows, baskets, utensils, boats, bows, ceremonials, and the most of the movable things that constitute material culture are artifacts.

Archaeologist.—An archaeologist is one who deals with the material side of the culture of the prehistoric period. Archaeology is prehistory. Besides studying artifacts the archaeologist investigates such things as ruins, earthworks, inscriptions, roads, trails, cemeteries and their contents. The archaeologist together with the ethnologist makes out time relations and attempts to correlate the ancient past with the written records of the historian.

In the study of archaeology the remarks of O. S. G. Crawford[8] are particularly pertinent: "The subject mat-

[8] Man and His Past, p. 38.

ter of archaeology consists mainly of pots and potsherds, stones, bones, and earthworks. The archaeologist's principal implement is the spade.'' One is interested in the objects brought to light by the spade not because of any intrinsic value but because by them may be traced the passage of man across the stage of development from a period without written records into a period with them. Real history varies only in the method of writing. In the early period, without the intent of its being a record and oftentimes all the more truthful for that, the writing is in the chipping of flints, the shaping of stones, the ornamentation of pottery, the refuse from 'kitchens,' defences in times of war, dwelling sites in times of peace, the burying of the dead, the erection of earth and stone altars for purposes of worship. The period of written record does not put an end to the unwritten, but adds minutiae and details and is capable of being read in printed pages instead of in the field or museum. The unwritten record requires a translator who understands its alphabet and an interpreter who can read its meaning. In a certain and very definite sense the archaeologist must prepare some of the material for the professional historian.

Anthropology.—Anthropology includes all the sciences that appertain to man, archaeology, ethnology, origin, dispersions, history; in a word, it is the study of man as an animal and as a rational being. Anthropology overlaps, on one side, the science of psychology and upon the other side it includes a good part of sociology.

Ethnology.—That part of anthropology that describes the customs and institutions, including mental, moral and physical characteristics, of the various groups of mankind is called ethnology.

Ethnography.—A consideration of the different families and races of people as they are distributed over the earth's surface constitutes ethnography.

Duty of the State.—The state should be interested in investigating its archaeological resources with such intelligence as will make them of real educational value. An archaeological survey is fundamental. An archaeological survey should cover, broadly, all aspects of the problem of the aborigines. It is an inventory of useful resources and is an exceedingly important part of the conservation work of the state. Reports of such a survey, as it progresses, should be published from time to time until, finally, a reasonably full and final resume could be embodied in an atlas with maps of the different counties.

Language groups.—Mankind can be divided into groups according to their languages, although similarity of speech among peoples must not lead to the conclusion that they are necessarily "blood relatives." The language stock that occupied the greatest extent of territory of all the American stocks was the Algonquian family. Their area reached from the Gulf of St. Lawrence to the Rocky Mountains; the Great Lakes are about in the center of their former distribution. The Algonquian language group, the name of which was adopted from the Algonkin tribe formerly living in Canada east of the present city of Ottawa, included perhaps a hundred tribes.

The Ojibwa or Chippewa, Ottawa, Menominee, Miami, Sauk, Mascoutin, Potawatomi, Foxes, and many others, so familiar to students of early history, were Algonquian. These tribes probably did not appreciate their language affinities any more than persons speaking English necessarily appreciate their language affinities with German. The affiliation of languages is very important because it indicates that at some time in the past one language was an offshoot from another or that the two had a common source of derivation. The lines of language development can often be clearly traced historically and made to show the paths that have been traveled in their dispersions.

The Algonquian tribes were often at war among themselves, frequently continuing until the stronger tribes completely exterminated the weaker ones. It transpired, however, in spite of their inter-tribal quarrels, that they sometimes united to defend their grounds against a common enemy. No doubt federations and disintegrations were going on, more or less constantly, after the population of the continent became numerous.

The Iroquois were another linguistic family. Their culture center was, perhaps, in the state of New York, but they occupied both the shores of Lake Ontario and of the St. Lawrence River. The stronger Iroquois tribes formed a compact against the weaker ones of their own group and carried their aggressive campaigns far into the Algonquian territory, even coming into Michigan.

If one will study the language groups analytically, he will observe more or less distinct peculiarities. A trained archaeologist can frequently make a distinction as to whether relics were made by one or another of the general divisions of tribes. Reference to this is made elsewhere.

CHAPTER IV

THE VALUE OF INDIAN RELICS

Necessity for Detail in Records. Any piece of handi-work made by primitive man is interesting and has a lesson to teach, provided its history is known. The history of a specimen should include the circumstances of finding and a description of the situation it was in when discovered. The place, and the relation of the piece to other objects when found, enter into the history. It should be stated whether the specimen was a surface find or imbedded in the soil. If it was found below the surface, mention should be made of the immediate surroundings, if at all unusual. Photographs are truthful in portraying original settings but they must be taken before the object is disturbed. Other artifacts, bones, and pieces of fire-broken stones lying in the immediate vicinity add greatly to a record, if note is made of them. Pieces found in association with others give clues to an understanding of all the circumstances under which they were lost or buried.

The common collector is sometimes almost a fanatic in the possession of some elegantly wrought pieces of flint, copper, pottery, slate, shell or stone. Truck of that kind is almost always stored in cabinets without either label or data and the owner is in perfect ignorance as to histories, delighting only in the variety and elegance of his specimens. A miscellaneous bagful of old clock wheels and sewing machine shuttles is just as valuable as such a collection. Neither has any merit except that it indicates what 'funny things' can be made by somebody; no one knows where they were made nor why they are different except that one is a wheel and another a shuttle. The value of a collection consists in its cataloguing, not in the specimens. The truthfulness underlying a catalogue and the labels represent the merit of a collection, but catalogues and data can be 'faked' as well as specimens. Care must be exercised not to be deceived by such crimes. It must be constantly borne in mind that the collecting of antiques and relics is not archaeology.

"Properly conducted excavations alone will yield satisfactory new material for study. . . . Many excavations, in which the harvest was enviably rich, have been made worse than useless by the unscientific way in which they have been conducted. Excavations should be carried on for the purpose of finding facts."[9]

Every Authenticated Relic is a Part of the Record of some Human Activity. In a sense, every specimen is a letter or a word; when enough words are assembled to make chapters, the chapters can be built into man's prehistory. To put all arrow heads, pottery, sherds, and other objects together, regardless of the sites from which they came, in a 'collection' is but assembling a boxful of unidentified pieces, worthless in archaeology. Such a mixture determines nothing.

Specimens of pottery, whole or in fragments, are valuable because their texture and particularly their patterns may identify them with certain localities and certain tribes as makers. For example, Algonquian pottery differs from pottery made by the Iroquois particularly in the rims and decorations. The Iroquois are known to

[9] R. A. S. Macalister, Textbook of European Archaeology, p. 15.

have come into Michigan, and certain sites, as those in Ogemaw County, have been attributed to them, but upon inadequate data. It is an interesting local problem to confirm or negate this claim, and it will be done, probably, by comparison of pottery fragments. Of course, the large and perfect pieces have been picked away, but enough may yet be found to decide the question.

Collectors, by reporting and comparing their specimens one with another, can aid greatly in determining culture areas. If it can be decided where particular types are the most numerous and where they are the scarcest, until a limit is found beyond which there are none at all, except sporadic misplacements, a culture area can be mapped out with reference to that type. Where the type is the most numerous would be its 'culture center.' An attempt has been made to determine the bird-stone area, for example. Such effort is constructive and scientific, but promiscuity and lack of classification are unscientific. Archaeology must proceed upon scientific lines, and science can have nothing to do with the haphazard.

Relics may be classified according to: (a) material, as bone, stone, shell, ivory, wood, flint, hematite, clay, etc.; (b) method of making, as by pecking, hammering, flaking, grinding, scraping, boring, etc.; (c) use, as woodworking, digging, fishing, sewing, hammering, harvesting, domestic work, hunting, warfare, ornament, etc.; (d) ceremonial; and, most inclusive of all, (e) 'problematical.'

From "State Archaeological Surveys," National Research Council, the following is pertinent: "In the first place, a collector should give chief attention to one locality or section. A desultory collection is too scattering to be of scientific value; but one confined to a restricted area will stand as a distinct unit and an index to the culture of its pre-historic inhabitants. One of the most satisfactory collections ever noted by the writer was from a single farm of 320 acres, the precise locations in which were recorded for each specimen.''

A moral obligation rests upon collectors. The relics, which are kinds of records left by early man, are all too few, but the assembling and collection of Indian relics is not an end nor an attainment within itself. Collections are of great use, however, in the larger field of interpreting the stages of human progress. The American Indian's chapter is closed so far as it indicates to what stages of civilization he might have arrived. But, by parallelism, we can infer that our own line of ancestry experienced the same grades of culture that he was going through and the history of humanity is enriched by comparisons.

Relics have value only when used as aids in interpreting some human problem. Aside from their relations to man's activities and modes of life, they lose intrinsic merit. The student of relics is an archaeologist and when he makes them instrumental in solving some phase of culture he becomes an anthropologist. The ideal of both is to discover phases of human activities and to weave facts, item by item, into an explanation of the changes in industry and behavior.

Relics may be described as movable and immovable. Those that can be gathered into collections and assembled into museums constitute the first class. The other class, and perhaps the more important, are those that are built up from, or dug into, the soil. These must be preserved from vandals, road building, plowing, weathering and the wear and tear of nature, and studied where they are. Any one who has an Indian work upon his premises should be as proud and careful of it as the most enthusiastic collector is of his copper, ceremonials, pottery, and other cabinet rarities. Private collectors will look after their specimens. A mound, as a part of the soil, is real estate, a stone axe is personal property, and can be transported at will. Probably nothing but state legislation will preserve any great number of our remaining earthworks.

CHAPTER V

EARTHWORKS

Mounds

Undoubtedly, mound building antedates the historic tribes. At least, it antedates the time when the tribes were located as they are known historically. Mounds are so conspicuous in some parts of the country that the term 'mound culture' may very properly be applied to the industry of the Indians who built them. The mounds of the Grand River Valley bear striking resemblances both in structure and contents to many mounds in Ohio and the South. The same may be said of other Michigan groups. One of the problems that awaits investigation is the tracing of the northern limit of this culture. No doubt numerous tribes constructed mounds, but many of them built so indifferently that their structures do not stand out prominently among their relics. The Chippewas, Potawatomi, perhaps the Mascoutins, and others, built small tumuli or threw up low banks of earth over their dead.

There is a group of fine mounds still standing below Grand Rapids upon the first terrace of the river bank. Mr. Hubbard[10] refers to them at some length. He explored a few of them but restored those that he disturbed to their original shape. When the writer visited the group in the summer of 1923 he observed that vandals had not kept their hands off. One of the mounds had

[10] Memorials of a Half-Century, p. 206.

recently been ditched through and the earth not replaced. It is a rule in archaeological ethics to replace all earth and stones not desired as specimens to their original positions after an examination has been made. Until quite recently, the only mound in the state preserved by either public or private enterprise is the one in Bronson Park, Kalamazoo. It is said that the mounds below Grand Rapids, referred to above, whose destruction has been imminent, are to be incorporated into the city park system.

There are two mounds on the larger of the Dickson lakes, near Brethren, Manistee County. One mound, situated on the S. E. ¼ of the S. W. ¼ of Section 10, W. half of Dickson Twp., measures fifty-three feet from trench to trench east and west by forty-one feet north and south. The surrounding trench, a feature not always associated with Michigan mounds, is thirty to thirty-six inches deep at the present time and must have been deeper when constructed. The mound has been extensively dug into by relic-hunters and other vandals but is still at least seventy-two inches high; it would be at least ten or more feet high if it had not been tampered with. A stump, charred by fire and without its bark, is rooted in the north slope and measures forty-two inches across. The other mound, in the N. E. ¼ of the N. W. ¼ of Section 15, on the eastern shore of the lakes is, if anything, slightly larger. It will be seen that these mounds compare very favorably with the Grand River groups and indicate a possibility of the extension of that culture to the Manistee River area.

Mr. Hubbard[11] states: "An instance of a similar construction is reported to me by Mr. Day, of Romeo,

[11] Memorials of a Half-Century, p. 201.

associated with the ancient remains of Macomb County. He says: 'In several places in this vicinity were found mounds made of stones, nicely piled up to a height of four or five feet, like a hay cock. They were entirely alone, and more than a mile distant from the group of earth-mounds elsewhere mentioned. One of these stone-mounds was opened forty years ago. It was four feet in height and placed in a circular excavation of two feet depth by four feet diameter. These stones were nicely placed, and had been preserved in shape by a tree which grew on the summit, and threw its roots over the sides of the pile. The stones being removed, portions of a human skeleton were exhumed.' ''

Schoolcraft reports that stone piles similar to those of Macomb County once existed upon Mackinac Island.

Mr. W. L. Coffinberry,[12] reporting upon Grand River mounds, speaks of eight groups, consisting, in all, of forty-six mounds. He says: ''The mounds examined vary from two feet to fifteen and one-half feet in height, and from ten feet to one hundred and two feet in diameter.'' Materials found were human remains, fabrics, pottery and drinking vessels, stone implements, bone implements, and copper implements. Where human remains were wanting nothing was found, while in no case were skeletons exhumed without revealing something else of interest, often all the varieties mentioned above. The pottery reported as found by Mr. Coffinberry was of different models: there were, at least, two distinct types of modeling. This marked difference in the pottery may indicate different agencies in the building or a coming together of two different shades of culture. Nothing of recent deposit was found in what is known as the

[12] Proc. Amer. Assoc. Adv. Sci., 1875, pp. 293–297.

Norton Group, a typical group of seventeen mounds about three miles below the city of Grand Rapids.

One particular mound, about twelve miles from the mouth of Grand River, in Ottawa County, appears to have been, from the description, of the nature of a shell heap or kitchen midden. It was entirely removed years ago to make way for a saw mill dock. It is described as a huge pile of ashes, shells, and fish bones, about fifteen feet high, forty-five feet wide and one hundred feet long and, in part, recent. This description is too vague to warrant one in concluding it to have been of ancient construction, although it may have been. It is a little difficult to reconstruct a mound after the earth it contained has been distributed for miles in making 'fills' and for road building, especially if the notes upon it are fifty years old.

According to Mr. Hubbard, who appears to have been a careful observer, the Great Mound of the Rouge River, at Delray, was an imposing structure several hundred feet long and forty feet high. It probably was a small natural hill added to with successive layers of earth by various workers at different times. It contained skeletons deposited in different positions: sitting, supine, and bent; bones of men, women, and children dumped without formality; burned bones, ashes of bones, and detached pieces. There were found in it some of the perforated skulls so peculiar to Michigan. Skeletons were found at all depths from ten feet below the natural surface of the surrounding soil to the top. It appeared to have been somewhat stratified with layers or pockets of different colored soils, ashes, charcoal, etc. It was probably, in later times, a central burial place for Indians coming long distances with the bones of their dead for interment, a kind of communal cemetery. The lower part of the mound must have been built before historic times. As late as the time of Pontiac, this elevation which commanded a view of several miles, up, down, and across the Detroit River, was a rendezvous. In the vicinity were other mounds of considerable size and "rich" in skeletons. One mound still remains inside the grounds of Fort Wayne.

According to Jesuit Relations, 1636, the Hurons in Canada, before their dispersal by the Iroquois, had the custom of depositing their dead in a common grave and building above them a funeral mound. Every ten or twelve years this ceremony took place. Mr. Hubbard forcefully suggests that a part of the interments upon the Rouge may have been made, according to this custom, by the Wyandotts, who were Huronic refugees driven from Canada by the Iroquoian invasion, and known to have settled south of Detroit where they have left a place name for a town.

Mr. H. D. Post[13] describes groups of mounds and inclosures upon Rabbit River, Allegan County. The inclosures were, some of them, very close together and none as much as two hundred feet across. Many of them were quite remote from water and showed little evidence of having been occupied. In the same vicinity were mounds surrounded by circles. Some of the numerous mounds of that county have been explored with road scrapers and horses. Such is the method of the relic hunter.

There are authenticated records of over six hundred mounds and tumuli in the state. This count is by no means final as the survey has not been thorough. Probably more than five hundred mounds have been

13 Michigan Pioneer Collections, Vol. III, p. 297.

destroyed. A triangle having for its base the southern boundary of the state with its apex at the head of Saginaw Bay will include the greatest number of mounds so far as the charts at present show. Clinton County has the largest number, fifty-seven; Lenawee, fifty-one; Kent, forty-six. New records are being reported every few days.

Whenever pieces of iron, copper and brass kettles, glass beads, crosses, and other trinkets of similar character are found in graves and hummocks of earth, the evidence is conclusive that the deposits had been made since the Whites, from whom the articles had been obtained, came into the region. Such finds, while telling instructive stories because they indicate the nationality of the people with whom contact had been made, have not so much interest for one studying unmixed Indian culture. Crosses are frequently unearthed with Indian bones and signify that a Catholic missionary, probably a Frenchman, had been in the country. Iron hatchets and kettles usually bear some kind of a trade-mark which reveals that they were made by an Englishman, a Frenchman, or a Dutchman.

If one will consult the invoices of goods[14] sent from government headquarters at Montreal to the Indians at Michillimackinac for the year 1782 he will observe that there were issued, among very many other things, silver arm and wrist bands, ear and finger rings, buckles, gorgets, moons, wheels and double silver hangers, besides tomahawks, half-axes, kettles, etc. According to their ancient custom of burying belongings of an individual with his body, these articles found their way into In-

[14] Refer to Michigan Pioneer Collections, X, for copies of various invoices, etc.

dians' graves for us to exhume and place in our collections.

One of the urgent problems in local research is the classification of mounds and the determination of their places chronologically or in time sequence. The fact is usually overlooked by heedless mound diggers that the mound itself is the important specimen. What it contains is complementary. The mound and its contents make the unit of discovery.

INCLOSURES AND EMBANKMENTS

Inclosures. Widely distributed throughout the country are evidences that man has busied himself at times by inclosing open spaces with banks of earth. Some of the inclosures bear evidence of considerable age. They may be as old as the oldest mounds. Mounds are situated inside some of them. Others were built since the discovery and are matters of historic record. Many of these earthworks are imposing in proportions, having banks from twenty to thirty feet high. The largest inclosure in the United States is that called Fort Ancient, in Warren County, Ohio. The distance around the crest of the irregular walls of Fort Ancient is nearly three miles. The space enclosed aggregates about one hundred acres. The height from the bottom of the moat to the crest is over twenty-five feet in many places.

The Indians of Michigan never undertook any such stupendous enterprise as Fort Ancient. There were, however, in this state many inclosures of striking appearance and outline. Inclosures are usually referred to as ''forts,'' on the supposition that they could have been built for no other purpose than that of defense.

There were at least two distinct patterns of forts. One type had curved walls, forming elliptical or circular spaces. The other type had nearly straight lines and sharp angles outlining irregular polygons. One might say that the two types are so different as to belong to quite different cultural conceptions.

A large number of our forts (like the garden beds) have been plowed down or mutilated beyond recognition. Ir an archaeological survey of the state the remaining works of this character should receive attention. They should be accurately located, measured, pictured, plotted and charted. We can give an approximately accurate description of one or two of the forts as they are today.

Missaukee Preserve. In the summer of 1923 an interested and enterprising gentleman gave the University of Michigan a tract of one hundred and twenty acres, situated in Section 14, Aetna Township, Missaukee County, upon which two well preserved inclosures are to be found.

The Surveyor of Missaukee County made the sketches that are upon a following page. ''The elevation of the embankments of the circles on the outside averages five and five tenths feet. The width on top of embankments is seven feet.''

There is a pine stump standing upon the crest of one of the walls which is forty-seven inches in diameter inside the bark. The number of annular rings per inch is ten or twelve. There are stumps nearly as large as this standing inside the inclosure. It has been fifty years, probably, since the trees were cut. From this it is fairly safe to estimate that at least two hundred and fifty years have elapsed since the forts were abandoned. How long they had been abandoned before this particular tree began to grow is, of course, purely conjectural. The same is true of the duration of the fort's occupation and the time of its construction.

The fact that the surface within the inclosure was strewn with hundreds of pottery fragments leads to the conjecture that it was occupied for a considerable time. Many small sherds may be picked up there now, though it would appear that all relics which might give important clues have been taken away. Pipes, whole pottery vessels, and other interesting artifacts are reported to have been found in or near the forts. A small mound nearby also yielded a skeleton and artifacts.

These interesting inclosures are now, almost too late, rescued from further spoliation by purchase and are available for scientific scrutiny. It remains to make careful examinations of them to determine, if possible, whether the banks were ever palisaded, as were some similar structures elsewhere located. The molds of decayed posts may be found as evidence that the inclosures with their walls heightened by a sort of post-fence upon the top were defenses against enemies. If the evidence in favor of fortification does not become reasonably convincing after careful investigation, other guesses as to the purpose to which they may have been put will be mentioned in speaking of the forts upon Rifle River in Ogemaw County. There is much similarity between the two groups of inclosures.

There is no stream or body of water within several miles of this inclosure except a small rivulet a mile away. Near Fort Number 2 there is a spring which, when the forest was standing, must have been perennial. It was trickling into a pool about thirty feet across in early summer; by late summer the pool was dried up. There are other small springs upon the tract.

The two forts are not upon an eminence, but from a quarter to a half mile away there is a range of low, gravelly hills, skirting the area upon all sides. It will be recalled that the entire country, parts of which we are describing, is of glacial drift.

In connection with the two forts described at length above, mention should be made of a third one located during the summer of 1924 by members of the museum staff. Fort Number 3 is found about six miles west by south of the Aetna Township forts, in the S. W. ¼ of the S. E. ¼ of Section 26, Reider Township, Missaukee County. It is approximately circular, one hundred and sixty-five feet in north and south diameter by one hundred and sixty feet east and west. There is a moat about the outside of the embankment, the walls rising from five to eight feet above its bottom. There were numerous rumors of another earthwork in the same vicinity, of horseshoe shape; and of another fort formerly existent near the village of Falmouth, but it was impossible to discover tangible verification of these statements.

Not far distant from the Reider fort there are a number of problematical earthworks, that cannot be included in the class of inclosures. They are raised perhaps three feet above the surrounding earth and range from forty to one hundred and eighty feet long, of no distinctive shape or appearance and not striking to the eye. The largest one is separated from the cluster of five by about a half mile of brush and is four hundred and fifty feet long. It winds irregularly over the surface of the ground and might be likened to a serpentine figure. That it is an effigy construction of some such nature is the simplest conjecture. It by no means follows that such a concept was present in the minds of the builders.

Hudson[15] answers the query of a Wiltshire peasant as to the curves in an ancient earthwork there, pertinently, for us: "I could only suggest in reply that it was no doubt a very ancient earthwork, dating back to the time when metal tools were unknown in England and that the chalk had been scooped up with sharp flints; that when they came to a very hard bit they had to make a bend to get round it . . ." Most of the earthworks of Michigan were constructed in the forest, amidst clumps of large trees difficult for the savage to cut down. It may be surmised that many of their irregularities are due to the presence of large trees and similar obstacles more easily gone around than removed.

The Rifle River Forts. Directly east from the Missaukee Preserve, across Roscommon County, lies Ogemaw County. Through the center of Ogemaw County flows Rifle River which empties into Saginaw Bay. As one crosses Roscommon County he hears of mounds, forts, graves, relics, etc.; all of which come within the scope of the state archaeological survey. At the crossing of one of the main roads, ten miles east of West Branch, and the Rifle River, is the hamlet of Selkirk, in the township of Churchill. Churchill is in the same tier of townships as Aetna, in Missaukee County, forty miles away.

Within a mile and a half of Selkirk are four inclosures; two north, or up the river; the other two down the river. This location is northwest from the north shore of Saginaw Bay. It is about fifteen miles from the southeast corner of Ogemaw County to the northeast shore of the bay. Iosco County lies between Ogemaw and the shore of Lake Huron. Churchill is the sixth township west of the Huron shore.

15 The Book of the Naturalist, p. 324.

In the Twelfth Report of the Bureau of Ethnology, 1890–91, an account of the Rifle River forts, Michigan, is given by Cyrus Thomas. In the Smithsonian Report, 1884, is an article by Mr. M. L. Leach entitled, "Ancient Forts in Ogemaw County, Michigan." In a leaflet by Mr. Harlan I. Smith, reference is made to the "works." No references to the Ogemaw "forts," excepting those borrowed from the older records, have come to the attention of the writer since the publications referred to above.

Being in doubt as to whether or not the inclosures had met the usual fate of the greater number of the state's immovable antiquities, the staff of the University Museum had for some time contemplated a visit to the Ogemaw district. On July 28, 1923, a party visited the Rifle River Valley for the purpose of obtaining first-hand information. The ultimate object was to have thorough investigations made in the hope that some of the secrets of the situation might be cleared up and, proportionately, conjectures reduced to lower terms.

The range of counties of which Ogemaw is one is a typical 'chopped over' and 'burnt over' district of north-central Michigan. The Rifle River is a beautiful clear-water stream of rapid descent over a cobble-stone bottom. Originally, it abounded in trout and such other fish as thrive in cool, clear eddies and occasional deep places. The dense forest was mostly pine, of excellent quality. The land surface is undulating with gravelly or sandy soil and glacial boulders are plentiful. Many fine lakes are to be found within the county but none are nearer the forts than six or seven miles.

Swamps are not large nor common in the vicinity. For the most part the river bank is firm, though with an occasional marshy strip. Many springs trickle from the margins of the low banks. Much of the land here has lapsed to the state on account of delinquent taxes, as it is of very poor quality; a great part of it is uninclosed and not worth the fencing. Occasionally a productive farm is to be observed, and a great many unproductive ones are occupied by rugged farmers, many of whom were at one time 'lumber-jacks.'

Reference is made in the report of Mr. Thomas to ''five inclosures commonly known as 'Indian Forts'; three on the east side and two on the west side of the river.'' We were unable to locate more than four and believe the report to be in error in this regard, although at a distance of fifteen miles west of southwest is an authenticated crescent whose exact location is in the center of the boundary between Sections 33 and 34, West Branch Township. It is presumably the Hauptmann work described in the old record. It is not upon a stream of any size. Its distance from a small branch of Mansfield Creek is, perhaps, fifty rods.

Inclosure Number 1 is well described in the diagram in Mr. Thomas' report. He states that at the time of his examination the area was heavily timbered with hemlock. At present the ground is nearly bare excepting numerous pine stumps upon the walls and within the enclosed space. The work itself appears to be in about the same condition as it was when his survey was made. Intelligent residents of the neighborhood say it is somewhat reduced by weathering and by cow-paths. Fortunately, the slashing in which this and the three other inclosures are located has never been damaged by cultivation.

The pathways leading from the openings of nearly all the inclosures are quite narrow and consist of the orig-

inal earth that was not disturbed in digging the trenches.
Originally, they had, perhaps, permitted two persons,
walking side by side, to pass through them. In one or
two places the gateways are as much as twelve feet in
width, as Thomas has indicated in regard to Number 1.
We were not able to verify the reports as to the number
of openings in the inclosures. Inclosure Number 2 might
have had five, but we were led to think that there were
only four places for entrance. Time and cows' feet have
wrought changes. Number 2 is the largest of the group,
being approximately three hundred feet east and west
by two hundred and eighty feet north and south. The
walls and moat are, for the most part, distinctly traceable. For long reaches the wall is seven or eight feet
slant height from the top to the bottom of the moat. The
trenches end abruptly at the gateways. Leach, in describing Number 3, indicates eight openings, one for each
cardinal and one for each intermediate point of the compass. This we were unable to verify, either as to points
of number or orientation. At present but four openings
are clearly apparent, one or two of them quite wide.
Upon the river side of the inclosure, lumbermen, seeking an approach to the river, have probably graded down
a space of thirty feet. The surface inside is rough and
uneven with hummocks three to six feet in height. Some
filling in and tearing down may have been done elsewhere, but such alterations can be detected and restorations can be made with a little skillful attention. Upon
the whole, the wonder is that all the works are so well
preserved.

Inclosure Number 4 is not completed. It is situated
upon the west side of the river and is more rectangular
in outline than the others, with an open side of two hun-

dred and six feet facing a narrow swamp lying between it and the stream. It has a narrow opening in the southwest corner and also one very near to the northeast corner. From the east end of the south wall to the middle of the first opening, the distance is one hundred and twenty-eight feet; from there to the second opening, one hundred and ten feet. From the second opening to the end of the north wall the distance is one hundred and sixty-two feet, making four hundred feet of earth construction in all.

Inquiry along the Rifle River brought nothing but negative answers as to whether arrows, hammer-stones, celts, axes, copper, or pottery had ever been unearthed. In almost every locality of the state many residents have a few specimens they have gathered in the fields. We were unable to find any specimens about Selkirk or to secure information about those who have them. The inclosures of Missaukee County were strewn with pottery fragments. The surface within and without the Ogemaw 'works' did not disclose a single specimen, although more searching and continued observation might bring some to light. No graves or mounds have been reported and much of the land has at some time been worked over. After several hours' search, a few pieces of pottery were found an inch or two below the surface, in two of the inclosures. We could, no doubt, have found more; but they are far from common.

The works we have been describing are very much like those which are attributed to the Iroquois of western New York and southern Canada. It is well known that those Indians made frequent forays into this section, but the specimens of pottery we have obtained are pronounced by competent ceramists to be Algonquian. No evidence of pit holes, fire-rings, or wigwam sites were found, excepting one small pit upon the inner side of bank Number 2. This pit, after considerable search, revealed nothing in the way of evidence as to the purpose for which it was made. It will be recalled that near the Missaukee works, pits are abundant. A number of skeletons have also been exhumed in that neighborhood. No finds of this description have been reported from the Rifle River district. This lack of finds, though not very convincing, may be accepted as evidence that the places were not occupied for any great length of time. There must have been burials, and artifacts will probably still be discovered. From the appearance of the stumpage, the Missaukee group and the Rifle River group must have been vacated at about the same time.

Inclosures in Other Parts of the State. The forts of the north-central part of the state are not, by any means, the only ones, but they happen to be the best preserved. In Climax Township, Kalamazoo County, was a perfect, elliptical inclosure, with major and minor axes of three hundred and thirty and two hundred and ten feet respectively. The walls were three feet high and the surrounding ditch ten or twelve feet wide.

Lanman[16] says: "The so-called 'forts' are but seldom met with and are fairly uniformly of small dimensions, the principal ones being in the southeast, along the shores of the Detroit, Huron, and Raisin Rivers; and occasionally upon Lake Erie, between the Detroit and Maumee Rivers." Upon what evidence he makes this statement is not known, but there is no apparent reason for doubting what he says about the southeastern part of the state, although the visible proof is lacking. If the

[16] Red Book of Michigan, 1871, p. 189.

reports, many of them vague, are to be given much credence, the entire state was pretty well 'fortified.'

Evidently taking Mr. Bela Hubbard as his authority, although he does not say so, Lanman reports further: "In the County of Wayne, on the north bank of the Detroit River, is a fort of the circular or elliptical kind, with an embankment two or three feet in height and compassing, perhaps, one acre. On the east side, as one approaches the fort, there are two parallel embankments of earth, within a few feet of each other, rising four or five feet and crossing the swamp in a direct line toward the fort."

Earthworks of Irregular Outline. Works of irregular outline once existed in different parts of the state. John T. Blois,[17] whom everyone seems to quote as an authority, and from whom Lanman seems to have taken, word for word, his account of the Springwell works, says: "In Bruce Township, in Macomb County, on the north fork of the Clinton, are several . . . with ditch on the outside and including from two to ten acres, with entrances which evidently were gateways and a mound on the inside opposite each entrance." He says, further, that near the mouth of the Clinton River there were ancient works, representing a fortress, similar to those in Ohio and Indiana. Blois speaks of similar banks of earth near the village of Marshall, Calhoun County, and of others in Kalamazoo County.

For a detailed survey of forts in Bruce and Armada townships, see the report of Mr. George H. Cannon[18] upon pre-historic forts in Macomb County. One incloses

[17] Gazetteer of the State of Michigan, p. 168.
[18] Michigan Historical Collections, Vol. XXXVIII, p. 73.

an acre, another between one and two acres, and the largest three and a half acres. These works were built in straight lines, making at some corners obtuse angles, at others acute angles. The smallest inclosure had three openings, the other four.

There is a record of a peculiar construction upon the north bank of the Raisin River, in the northeast part of the village of Tecumseh, described by John J. Adam,[19] as follows: "It was laid out in the form of a square and circle, with an opening from one to the other where they joined . . . the trails all leading to and from the circle, and both parts having embankments of about four feet in height, and having in the center of the circular part a pit five or six feet deep . . . When the white settlers first came here there were some cedar posts in the outer embankment, and there were evidences of the place being quite often used for meetings or gatherings of some kind. . . ." This description would apply very well to some of the works in Ross County, Ohio, and to others found elsewhere in that state.

Near the village of Boone, Wexford County, on the N. W. $\frac{1}{4}$ of the S. E. $\frac{1}{4}$ of Section 22, Boone Township, is a remnant of what must have been once an extensive earthwork of an irregular shape, according to report, approximating the form of a horseshoe. Only about two hundred feet of the north arm of the work yet remains, the rest having succumbed to the plough and erosion. There were reports of two other earthworks of similar, though smaller design, near this construction and not over a mile away. On the days examination was made, these two works could not be found in the brush. They have been extensively dug into by the ubiquitous relic-

[19] Michigan Pioneer Collections, Vol. II, p. 363.

seeker and one has probably been ploughed down. A number of potsherds and some stone artifacts have been found on the sites.

Embankments, circles, squares, breastworks, and other forms of earth construction, not described as mounds, are reported also from Antrim, Branch, Huron, Kalkaska, Keweenaw, Osceola, Saginaw, St. Joseph, Sanilac, Tuscola, and Wexford counties; probably not half of them are recorded.

Many of the 'forts' are so small they could not have served as permanent places of abode for many people. Villages may have been located within larger ones, but most likely they were refuges for the people of the outlying districts in time of danger, as suggested by Bushnell.[20] If the inclosures were forts, which signifies warfare, there must have been two hostile groups in the territory at the same time. Whether they were the work of the invaders or the invaded, or both, gives opportunity for more theorizing.

There are those who think the inclosures have some ceremonial significance. If the inclosures were fortifications, why would they have so many openings? Primitive people were intensely religious and influenced by shamanistic magic. To perform rites and ceremonies, paraphernalia, including such as would shield performances from the public gaze, was necessary. Temporary and fragile lodges were used for performances. To make seclusion more secure and permanent, screens of earth might have been constructed, forming a kind of cabinet.

The places mentioned should all be measured accurately and sketched with instruments of precision in the

[20] Native Villages and Village Sites East of the Mississippi River. Bureau of Ethnology, Bull. 69, p. 18.

hands of competent surveyors. It often happens that a closed space appears to the casual observer as being of a pretty definite shape when, in reality, the conception is quite wrong in details. The 'stepping-off,' ten-foot pole, and the tape-line methods, supplemented by guess work, are not very accurate when irregular lines and angles are involved.

PIT HOLES

Perhaps the most numerous earth constructions are holes in the ground of varying depths and capacities. They are frequently overlooked because the casual observer or relic hunter is searching for something more conspicuous. The usual explanation of the pits is that they were used for storage, as farmers have 'root cellars.' The common term applied to storage pits in the ground is 'cache.' Sometimes ears or grains of corn that have withstood decay, perhaps for centuries, are found in them. Some show that they have been made for fires used in cooking, like a 'clam bake,' barbecue, or the lumbermen's 'bean holes.' Upon the Missaukee Preserve, near the inclosures, are hundreds of pits, many of them so close together that the rims overlap. Only one has been cleaned out with care. When they are examined under proper supervision more may be added to our knowledge of the general situation. One theory about the pits, when found in numbers and close together, is that they were 'fighting holes,' like the rifle pits used in modern warfare.

In July, 1924, representatives from the University Museum examined one of these pit holes. A ditch was dug around the pit to a depth of six feet, several inches below its bottom. The original hole went to a point with slanting sides like an inverted hollow cone. The soil was examined with great care. Nothing except a few small fragments of charcoal which might have fallen in from the burnt-over ground surface was found. There was no evidence that fire had ever been used in this pit. The shape precluded a bottom upon which even one person might have stood squarely upon both feet. A half-breed Indian living in the vicinity said the pits had been used by his ancestors as security for their women and children during a fight. The tapering of the sides of the pit to a point indicates that the aforesaid half-breed knew nothing about it, or his ancestors had a peculiar way of 'digging in' their families. If these pits upon the Preserve were for storage the wonder is what was stored in them. Certainly not corn or vegetable supplies, for the soil is so infertile that an acre of it could never have brought even a small quantity to maturity.

At Ada, in Kent County, there are numbers of pits similar to those so common elsewhere. At this location it is easy to conceive that there were large quantities of corn produced because the very fertile flood plain of the Thornapple River is near by.

Mr. Andrew Blackbird,[21] son of an Ottawa chief, in writing of his people says: "The mode of securing their corn was first to dry the ears by fire. When perfectly dry, they would then beat them with a flail and pick all the cobs out. The grain was then winnowed and put into sacks. These were put in the ground in a large cylinder made out of elm bark, set deep in the ground and made very dry, filling this cylinder full and then covering it to stay there for winter and summer use."

[21] History of the Ottawa and Chippewa Indians of Michigan, p. 32.

No doubt the Indians often made 'caches,' using them as ordinary granaries, repositories for food-stuffs and supplies, to be drawn upon as necessity required. They could have been roofed over with bark or other protective material against rain and storm and very well serve this purpose. Some, no doubt, were for hiding or secreting supplies against marauders.

There are in various places throughout the state so-called 'hut-rings,' ridges of earth thrown up in circles around wigwams as protection against cold. Similarly, in country places, modern houses are banked up to prevent freezing.

In the prehistoric mining district of Lake Superior there are to be seen pits for altogether another purpose from those mentioned. These were dug down to facilitate the securing of the metal. In other places there are 'diggings' where cherts for making implements were obtained. There is evidence of these about Saginaw Bay. When an archaeological survey of the state is made, we shall know more about these Indian workings, and curiosity and conjecture will give way to accurate knowledge.

Mr. Bela Hubbard,[22] on the testimony of a Mr. Henry Little, mentions a sunken circle or ditch two or three feet deep, without embankments, in Kalamazoo County. This excavated circle enclosed a space of an acre and a half; wonder has been expressed as to the disposition that was made of the soil that was removed. It brings to mind the intaglios of Wisconsin.

Garden Beds

Another conspicuous feature of Michigan's antiquities was the 'garden bed' construction. These sym-

[22] Memorials of a Half-Century, p. 205.

metrical, low, earth ridges were laid out with precision and showed much artistic conception in their
designs. Some were wheel-shaped with 'spokes' running
out to a circular ridge from a circle within, but most of
them were in well planned geometrical designs. They
resembled beds in a formal garden, hence the name.
They were of a different conception from the 'beds' and
cornfields found elsewhere. They may have been real
gardens, but the detail and accuracy of outline gives
them peculiar significance. Schoolcraft[23] describes them,
1827 and 1837, while they were "undisturbed parts of
the mixed forest and prairie lands" and says they may
indicate "field-husbandry" but classifies them, after all,
as enigmatical.

The garden beds of Michigan have been entirely destroyed, sad to relate. Had they been preserved, they
would to-day rank among America's striking relics of a
distinctive aboriginal trait, like the great serpent mound
of Ohio and the numerous effigies of Wisconsin. Beds
are reported to have been located in several counties east
from a line running from the south-western corner of
Berrien County to the head of Saginaw Bay. At least
twenty-three of them have been described. There were
also a few in Indiana. In extent, they varied from the
'wheel' of Kalamazoo, ninety feet in diameter, to rec-
tangles of over a hundred acres. Reference should be
made to Michigan Pioneer and Historical Collections,
Vols. II and XIV. Very good diagrams of a number of
plots have been preserved and the measurements of a
few are a matter of record. It is said the beds had the
appearance of being very old. Schoolcraft says several

[23] Historical and Statistical Information, Part I, D. Evidences of a Fixed Cultivation at an Antique Period, p. 54.

hundred years, basing his calculation upon the vegetable growth that stood upon and among them. Someone has suggested that they may have been the work of the Mascoutins, a tribe that disappeared from this region very early in historic times, but their authorship is nothing more than a guess and depends upon no more foundation than does the theory that the mounds of the Ohio Valley were built by the Cherokees.

Upon an island comprising ninety acres in the Kalamazoo River, six miles above the city of Kalamazoo, is a hill imagined by some to be an Indian mound. The hill rises abruptly fourteen feet from the level of the island, which is scarcely above the flood plain. The top of the hill is quite level. The outline of the elevation is triangular and upon it are six parallel shallow depressions or ditches running the entire distance of its longest axis, a hundred feet. These ditches are about fourteen inches deep and two or three feet wide. The ditches are twelve feet apart. One with some imagination and a not too critical attitude of mind might convince himself that here there is still remaining a small garden bed.

CHAPTER VI

TRAILS AND SITES

Trails. The trails or paths that the Indians habitually took in going from place to place are among the most valuable relics of their times. They are as interesting to study and trace as earthworks and village sites. Historically, they are of particular importance because very many of them were followed by the first white settlers and finally became main roads and routes of travel. Only seldom is it possible to find the real footworn track through the woods, but traces of trails that were followed can be made out for miles sometimes by the old surveys and from the records left by early writers. The trunk lines from Detroit to Chicago, from Detroit to the Saginaw country, and from Grand Rapids to St. Joseph are illustrations of the conversion of trails into modern 'improved' roads. Of course, as the roads are straightened, they depart from the original traces, but the general lines of direction are very close to the pathways the Indians trod for unnumbered years.

In regard to the origin of these trails, the handbook of American Indians, Bureau of American Ethnology, says: "Supplemental however to these open, and in times of war obviously dangerous routes (meaning water ways), were paths or trails, many of them originally made by the tracks of deer or buffalo in their seasonal migrations between feeding grounds or in search of water or salt licks. The constant passing over the same path year after year and generation after generation often so packed the soil that in places, especially on hillsides, the paths are still traceable by depressions in the grounds or by the absence of or the difference in vegetation.''

Some of the principal trackways were double paths, probably due to the original becoming so deep and worn as to be unserviceable in wet weather. Indians were migratory and went on long tramps, often coming back to the place of departure. Time was no object. Sometimes they made amazingly long journeys for the purposes of trade, to visit other tribes, to attend councils, or for making war. Under movement a group would march one behind another, hence our expression 'Indian file'.

In the selection of the route, the aborigine generally showed rare good judgment. He avoided steep declivities, took the shortest feasible cut, came in contact with rivers at the best fording places and if possible avoided stony, rough ground, brier thickets, and places of dense bush. High ground that was normally dry was generally selected.

In mountainous country, travelling bands followed the valleys and knew all the gaps. In fine, from a topographic standpoint, their route was such as an engineer would select if he were not hampered by the government system of rectangular surveys.

There was a notable trail from where Detroit now stands to the lower end of Lake Michigan and thence up the western shore of that lake to Green Bay, Wisconsin. Another great double trail commenced at what is now Toledo, Ohio, diagonally traversed the Lower Peninsula, passing several miles east of Kalamazoo, through Grand Rapids and thence to the Straits of Mackinac.

Another trail leading to the crossing at the Straits from the south started from Detroit, passed through Saginaw, and followed northerly along the west shore of Lake Huron.

There were secondary trails angling into the great trails like feeders. Besides the many main trails and their very numerous collaterals, there were hundreds of local paths leading from village to village, to hunting and fishing grounds, to corn fields, etc.

The Indian's trail was the pioneer's first highway. Those trails that became permanent roads can generally be identified by their disregard for the points of the compass. A highway that deviates greatly from the section lines will bear investigation to determine if it were not formerly an Indian path. For those who may wish to study trails it will be of interest to know that the former locations of these ancient highways can still be traced so that oftentimes a creditable map of them may be constructed.

There are numerous sources from which information may be obtained. The first, and probably the most trustworthy source, is the field-records of the United States Surveys. A Deputy U. S. Surveyor was instructed to note all Indian trails, their bearing, and also any Indian villages. A copy of these records is supposed to be on file in the office of the Register of Deeds for each county, but one will generally find such record in the office of the County Surveyor.

There are two sets of surveys to be consulted: one made by the surveyor who ran the section; and what is known as the interior lines. It frequently transpires that some of the early surveyors did not comply with the law in noting these data. In platting the distances, which are in chains and links, generally one cannot obtain a suitable scale. In order to reduce to feet, treat the links as a decimal of a chain and multiply by sixty-six. This will enable one to locate the point on a map.

Another source of information is county histories which sometimes give the location of some of the principal trails. Again, the papers in the Michigan Pioneer Collection furnish occasional bits of information. Old residents sometimes can recall land marks, traces of paths, and runways across farms with which they are familiar. Sometimes traces are still visible through original woods, across unplowed fields and slashings.

The best scale to use on a county map is one mile to an inch, or if the district has been covered by the U. S. Survey their topographical maps will do very well. The scale of these maps is nearly one mile to the inch. The original map one makes should be on tracing cloth in order to obtain blue prints which may be used in the field and exchanged with others. Eventually a collection of district or county maps that will be both dependable and valuable may be worked out through cooperation. For the foregoing suggestions upon trails the writer is indebted to Mr. Edward J. Stevens, Secretary of the Michigan State Archaeological Society.

Village and Camp Sites. Man is instinctively a social animal and has always lived in societies. In their very early history, according to some pre-historians, men lived in hunting packs. Later, as culture developed, they formed groups with more or less fixed abodes. The Indians assembled into villages. Of course, they were more or less nomadic, but seemed to range about and, from time to time, to return to places they had formerly occupied.

When they remained long in one place or returned occasionally to the same place, they left proof of it in fireplaces, broken implements, with once in a while a whole one lost by accident, rubbish, animal bones, potsherds, ash heaps, etc. Mounds were sometimes erected over dwellings, and dwellings were erected upon mounds. The only way old villages or camping places can be located is by findings such as these.

The Indians, in selecting a site, exercised the same discretion that we would. They needed a constant supply of water, a sheltered spot, dry soil, and plenty of fuel. The dwellings were removed from trees, whose trunks and branches might cause accidents in case of storms. The fire risk was considered also.

Sites may be found along rivers, particularly where confluent, above the flood plains, as at Three Rivers and along the Saginaw and Tittabawassee where branches come in. In Ionia County, upon a high eminence just below the village of Muir, at the junction of the Maple and Grand rivers, is a trench and an embankment, forty-eight rods long, still quite traceable—the defense of an old village. In fact, there is a double row of trenches at this point, one inside the other, forming a crescent-shaped barricade upon the rear, while the other side is sufficiently guarded by the steep bluff of the Maple River. This site is known, locally, as the Arthurburg Hill. There were very large villages on the St. Marie River. Where hunting and fishing were good or where the soil was adapted to their crude agriculture, Indians settled down for considerable periods. Agriculture conduced to steady habits.

Mr. Fred Dustin, who has made extended investigations in the Saginaw Valley, speaking of Saginaw

County, says: There is little doubt in my mind that the number of villages in this county exceed a hundred.'' The region of Saginaw Bay and of the valley drained by the Saginaw River was probably the most thickly populated section of the state. Throughout that section Indian antiquities of all kinds are very abundant.

It is very likely that many of the inclosures referred to elsewhere were village sites. The description, quoted by Bushnell[24] from Pere Sebastien Rasles of villages in Quebec, perhaps describes fairly accurately some of the sites of this state: '' 'Their cabins are very quickly set up; they plant their poles, which are joined at the top, and cover them with large sheets of bark. The fire is made in the middle of the cabin; they spread all around it mats of rushes, upon which they sit during the day and take their rest during the night.' (Rasles, (1), p. 135.)'' This is a very good description of a form of construction that had a wide distribution.

The size of Indian settlements is overestimated in the popular mind. There is no reason for believing there was ever an Indian population of as many as twenty thousand throughout the entire territory now included in the state of Michigan; fifteen thousand would probably be nearer the correct number. Putting the population at one time at eighteen thousand for the state there would be an average of two hundred and twelve per county. If half the counties were unoccupied, and no doubt many of them were very sparsely inhabited, there would then be but a few over four hundred for a county, who, if all assembled, would not make a very populous village. At times larger assemblies might have been pos-

[24] Native Villages and Village Sites East of the Mississippi River. Bureau of Ethnology, Bull. 69, p. 23.

sible, but not for very long periods because the means of subsistence for great numbers was not available. There is not a small town, even to-day, that would not starve to death were it not for ready means for transportation. A village with a thousand Indians remaining for six months would have been metropolitan.

It may be computed from estimates by Carl Kelsey[25] that in certain districts, by combining primitive agriculture with the chase, as did the Cherokee, Shawnee, and Iroquois, about sixty-five individuals could have subsisted in a township of thirty-six square miles. But that is the maximum limit and could not have obtained over the state at large, by any means. Perhaps the Saginaw Valley and a few other favorable sections could have carried that population load.

Burying Grounds. It is a kind of superstition that there is something sacred about the dead; but bones and skeletons are not sacred to the archaeologist whenever he can get his digging tools into ground that is supposed to contain human remains. When dead Indians are the objects of investigation the tokens that were buried with them are as much sought for as the skeletons. One of the evidences adduced to prove the belief of primitive man in a future life is the presence in his grave of articles which he was supposed to need in another world. The Algonquians, who laid down at least one stratum of our pre-history, were mystics and dreamers, but religion, aside from sacred objects connected with ceremony, is not a part of archaeology. A large number of artifacts that are reclaimed are grave finds. The plowman and ditch digger have brought more of them to light than the trained investigator.

[25] The Physical Basis of Society, p. 102.

As Indians had the social tendency to assemble into groups, so they collected their dead, as we do, in cemeteries. Burial places are usually discovered accidentally but may be looked for near village and camp sites. Every grave that comes under observation should be investigated systematically. Burials, as elsewhere noted, were often made in mounds, nearly all of which are monumental. Sometimes isolated graves are discovered. Frequently burials were made under floors of dwellings or near by. Many interments were made soon after death, and again, ossuaries are found where bones were placed after having been stripped of the soft parts. Skulls and other parts of skeletons are often missing in graves. Some interest attaches to the attitude in which the bodies were placed and to their orientation.

From evidence that Mr. Bela Hubbard gives, burning of bodies, or at least incineration of bones, was practiced by some of those who used the Springwell Mounds as burial grounds.

The following from "State Archaeological Surveys," National Research Council, is pertinent: "Graves are found singly or in groups and there are seldom surface indications. No grave should be explored unless it can be done thoroughly. That is, photographs taken as the work proceeds; the skeleton, whether whole or fragmentary, carefully dug into relief by use of hand trowels; and notes written as to the position of all objects. The bones should be carefully preserved. They will seldom break unless carelessly handled. If a bone is decayed, dig its entire length under it and take it out adhering to the clay and wrap it up carefully. If all the fragments of the skull are there save them all, as the skull can be restored later. Where one grave is found there may be others and a trench should be run in the direction in which the cemetery exists, a ground plan made, and all graves numbered. If it is a village site one should look for the ash pits. Ashes have a wonderful preservative quality and carbonized food, corn, seeds, cloth, mattings, and so forth, are frequently found. The ashes and black soil of fire pits should be most carefully examined.''

One of the best published statements of detailed procedure will be found in Arthur G. Parker's ''An Erie Indian Village and Burial Site,'' Bulletin 117 of the New York State Museum, Albany, New York.

Workshops. A workshop is easily recognized. It is a place where flinty spalls, flakes, rejects, and broken stone implements are found in great abundance within a small space. Chippers, hand hammers, and anvils are generally interspersed among the debris. More than likely, at such a place, some ancient arrow maker did his work. Often the crude material upon which he operated was brought from distant places. Again, in localities where the material existed naturally in the rock or soil, chipping was done close by. Blanks were frequently roughed out into leaf-shaped pieces at the source of supply and then taken home to be retouched into the desired finished shapes. Caches or hoards of such blanks are not infrequent and are described in another paragraph.

Arrow and spear heads that appear to be made of imported material are common. Ohio flint is well distributed throughout the state. Obsidian, which does not exist in the natural state this side of the Rocky Mountains, found its way here and beyond. Native flinty stone, suitable for chipping, is abundant in places, but most of it is not of very fine quality. Occasionally, a choice piece of 'float' material was found and made into some desired object. Without doubt, a large number of ready made implements were imported. We can not decide, always, whether those of non-native stuff were brought in as found or in the rough. Here is opportunity for fine distinction; if a piece is of a kind of workmanship not usual in the district, it is probably a foreign product. If the design is common and the tooling not unusual, it may have been made from blanks or the natural stones that were transported from far away places.

The cherts and flints of the state are generally drab of color, rather coarse grained and often contain fossils, blemishes and flaws, although a few beautifully banded or striated cherts with a play of colors are found. Along the Kawkawlin River, in Bay County, there were numbers of workshops where whole nodules, fragments in all stages of reduction, and finished specimens were abundant. The natural nodules found upon the Kawkawlin workshops and those of the Saginaw were probably transported from the shores of Saginaw Bay and from as far east as the head waters of the Cass.

Near Base Lake, in Washtenaw County, workshops present two types of material and chipping. Upon one of them the spalls and rejects are of an excellent quality of flint. Not fifty rods away from that shop was another where both the material and workmanship were of a very crude character. These shops were probably the places where two operators, each using a different kind of material from the other, and one more skillful than the other, worked at different times. The place where the cruder work was done one might conjecture was the older, especially if the corroborative testimony of other differences could be discovered.

Fine grained, gritty gray stone, similar to felsite and rhyolite but softer, was in general use for implements and some elegantly wrought spears of it are in collections. This goes to show that the skillful flaker did not always exert his best efforts upon only choice material.

Stones from which axes and celts were made are very abundant along banks of streams and lakes, and hard, water-worn, pieces of igneous rock suitable for axe making are plentiful over the surface of the ground. An axe has been made, as an experiment, in forty-five minutes, and a grooved, polished specimen of such material as granite and syenite in one and one-half hours by a white man employing only the stone tools and methods of the Indian axe maker. Mr. Charles E. Brown[26] says: ''In changing his place of residence from one camp site to another it was probably often more convenient for the Indian to leave his axe and other heavier stone implements behind and to make others when he arrived at his destination than to carry them with him. On the other hand, stone axes of good quality appear to have been often cherished by their owners.''

[26] Grooved Axes. Wisconsin Archaeologist, April, 1918, p. 2.

CHAPTER VII

CULTURE TRAITS

Hunting. Stealthily, soft of foot, and taking advantage, unconsciously, of color protection, the primitive hunters of Michigan sought the large game of the forest and plains. They employed many devices in rounding up deer, moose and elk, and the few buffalo which, perhaps, ranged through the southern part of the state.

When the hunter could make the approach, he shot game with bow and arrow. Deer and moose were also driven into the water and overtaken with canoes. Mr. Darius B. Cook,[27] in speaking of an Indian he knew, says: ''He prided himself on running down deer. Whenever he desired one, he took a track, followed it carefully until he started him, and then a steady trot, and in a short time would run down and cut his throat. This has been done by many a young Indian buck.'' Pitfalls and ingenious traps were some of the devices employed in securing game. One should consult Traps of the American Indians, by Mason, Smithsonian Report, 1901, and Indian Tribes of the Mississippi and Great Lakes, as described by Nicholas Perrot in the translation by Miss Blair, for details upon traps and hunting large game.

Beaver were much sought for fur and flesh. They were usually taken in the winter when their houses could be despoiled from the ice. Small animals were trapped. Dogs were used in coursing. Bears were formidable

[27] Six Months Among the Indians, p. 9.

animals to attack. Mr. Alanson Skinner[28] describes a
bear trap as follows: The dead-fall "was made of a heavy
log often weighted at the upper end with stones. The
log was set up obliquely and was supported by 'figure 4'
trigger. Directly under the log, a small enclosure of
stakes was built, in which the bait was placed. In order
to get at the lure the bear was obliged to enter the enclosure. The instant the bait was touched, the trigger
to which it was attached released the log, which crashed
down on the animal and broke his back."

When the hunting season came on, drives were organized with ceremony. The procuring of game was not a
sport, it was serious business, especially for those who
had not good supplies of wild rice and corn. A sufficient
catch of game stood between the hunters and starvation
during the winters.

When big game was sought the implements and methods of hunting and warfare were considerably alike, but
the pursuit of game was essential to existence and required continual effort. The forest and plains Indians
were constant hunters but occasional warriors. Since
there were so many streams and lakes frequented by
myriads of large wild fowl, especially during the migration seasons, hunters were attracted to them. No doubt,
the eggs of birds, like berries in season, contributed to
the food supply.

Many Indians were great fish eaters. Fish were
speared, hooked, 'gorged,' snared and taken in wiers,
nets and scoops. Hooks made of shell and copper that
were probably used in taking fish have been found on
old sites.

[28] Material Culture of the Menominii. Museum of the American Indian, p. 187.

Agriculture. Agriculture is a means of obtaining subsistence as is hunting, fishing, and gathering wild seeds and roots. It requires a steadier habit of life than nomadic hunting. The food plants cultivated by our Indians were Indian corn, beans, squashes, and perhaps melons and pumpkins, all indigenous to America. Tobacco was also cultivated but not as a 'food' plant.

For preparing the ground and its cultivation, specialized tools were invented. As such implements were mostly of wood, collections of relics in this region rarely contain real agricultural implements. Sometimes wide, thin, and long flint implements, supposed to have been attached to handles, are picked up. If they have notches at one end they are called 'hoes.' If there is no notching for holding a handle they are 'spades.' Spades and hoes of beautiful workmanship, as long as twenty inches and as wide of blade as twelve inches, are common in other states, particularly Illinois. Large clam shells made good digging tools. Flat bones of animals, such as shoulder blades, made excellent hoes when attached to handles.

There are found in places that have not been disturbed by the plow of the white man, corn hills distributed over areas of considerable extent. Mr. Edward A. Foot[29] says: "The oak-opening land in the south part of the county [Eaton] seemed better adapted to the Indian mode of life than the dark and heavily timbered forests north of here. Signs of corn-fields—rows of corn hills overgrown with turf—could be seen at an early day upon this prairie where Charlotte now stands.

"During the sugar-making season they could move into the heavy timber and camp among the great sugar maples."

[29] Michigan Pioneer Collections, Vol. III, p. 379.

Trade and Commerce. Exchange is a very old element of culture. It began in a stratum of society lower than that of the Indian. The archaeological evidences that the Indians were traders is abundant. In their old as well as in their recent graves, in mounds, upon camp sites and workshops are found materials not native to the state and artifacts not of local design. Thousands of large and small shells from the Gulf of Mexico, and perhaps some from other salt waters, have been collected. Some of the smaller ones are perforated to be strung as beads and the larger ones fashioned into ladles or etched for ornaments. Imported flints and stones have been referred to elsewhere.

Extensive traffic was carried on in perishable stuffs as furs, feathers, wooden contrivances like boats, paddles, etc. Indian economics had not developed a standard medium of exchange like money. Barter, or 'swapping,' was as far as he got in merchandising. Wampum is sometimes called 'Indian money' but it was not used as currency, although white traders in the eastern states are said to have made it a rough standard of values. For an illuminating treatise on wampum, one may consult The Functions of Wampum among the Eastern Algonkian, by Frank G. Speck (Memoirs of American Anthropological Association, Vol. VI, No. 1).

Barter with some tribes went farther than trade in commodities. Men negotiated for wives the same as we do for cows but usually with more ceremony. In this kind of trade, wampum, especially with the eastern tribes, entered into the transaction as a part of the ceremony rather than as part of the price.

The distribution of Michigan copper east, south, and west for hundreds of miles, is another proof that there were long lines of trade.

CULTURE TRAITS   103

Cadwallader Colden,[30] writing in 1755, says: "The Adirondacks formerly lived three hundred miles above the Trois Riviers where now the Utawawas are situated; at that time they employed themselves in hunting, and the Five Nations made planting of corn their business. By this means they became useful to each other, by exchanging corn for venison."

There are different ways for commodities to become distributed: one is by stealing, another is by rendering some kind of equivalent or by real trade. Capturing and confiscating by conquest in war is a kind of stealing. Where trade went on there must have been peace among the traders and along the lines of trade. If there were long lines of trade there must have been large districts where the tribes were living in comparative harmony among themselves, which goes to show, as stated in the paragraph upon warfare, that fighting and war were not the fundamental business among the Indians. There probably were tribes more active in trade than others. It is said that the Ottawas in Michigan particularly had the knack of trade. Just when the profession of peddling originated we cannot say, but it was far back in the evolution of commerce.

Warfare. In the popular conception the Indian was, first of all, a warrior. When we dismiss from mind the stories about the wars that are recorded in the white man's history and try to reconstruct Indian society as it was in the untainted stone-age period, there is little tangible material bearing upon his military affairs. Folk-lore and tradition—the stuff of which mythology is made—may be of some aid but it is not dependable for matters of cold fact.

[30] The History of the Five Nations of Canada, 3rd Ed., Vol. I, p. 22.

From archaeological evidence, we can deduce that periods of peace prevailed for long times over very large areas of territory because trade could not have prospered in a time of general fighting. On the other hand, it has been shown that different zones represent within themselves different culture traits, one following another, and prove fluctuation in population. There were migrations and counter currents. When one group attempted to dispossess another of its grounds, fighting probably took place. As has been indicated elsewhere, some wars had economic causes.

One wave of migrants, driven by a stronger force, pushed against the next, and so on, in lines of least resistance, until a wide expanse of country was in agitation. This has been observed in historic times and a safe analogy justifies the generalization.

Upon archaeological evidence, Parker[31] has traced the migration of the Iroquois from the south-west below the Ohio River into New York and Canada. When analytical, intensive studies like those of Parker and Skinner are undertaken in Michigan we shall have some definite knowledge of our Indian migrations.

The tools of warfare were bows and arrows for long range; clubs and mutilating hand weapons for close-up fighting. Skulls and large bones are once in a while dug up with flint arrow points still embedded in them. Scalping, probably developed from head-hunting, was much encouraged by the bounties offered by the French and English after they became embroiled in Indian affairs. It must have been a difficult task to cut and peel off the thick skin of a man's head with a flint knife. It

[31] The Archaeological History of New York. New York State Museum Bulletin, Nos. 235, 236, p. 96.

became easier with a steel knife and the reward was greater. Scalping in prehistoric times was probably confined to the eastern United States and lower St. Lawrence.

Indians were experts in ambuscade, which they used in trapping both foes and wild animals. They did not fight in battle array but were adroit bushwhackers. Always loyal to his immediate kinship, the brave considered treachery to an ally perfectly consistent with his ethics. In battles, non-combatants were not recognized; the aged, women, and children, took their chances with the success or failure of the war party to which they belonged. Women frequently took part in the actual fighting.

Prisoners and spies of war were frequently most cruelly dealt with. The sufferer at the stake, or pinioned to a tree or to the ground, while a slow death resulted from mutilations, fire, and ingenious, hellish devices, stoically taunted his persecutors that the same fate he was meeting would have been theirs if his party had been the victors.

It may have occurred that tribes went to war with the intent of securing additions to their own numbers. Captives were, many times, adopted into the tribe of the victors, thereby augmenting their numbers and strength. Usually the leaders and fiercest warriors of an enemy were put to death. The others were absorbed by the successful parties which strengthened themselves and depleted the vanquished. This system was quite successful when prisoners were brought from long distances. No doubt there were wars that resulted in complete extermination of tribes and culture traits. The tribes that the white men first met were the survivors out of hundreds that had disappeared from time to time through the thousands of years of struggle and contention. Several of them appeared to be upon the wane and others coming into ascendency.

Carpentry. The Indians, considering the nature of their tools, were good mechanics and developed the ability to work in woods. Evidence of this is both historical and indirect. As testimony to their dexterity, they have left many wood-working implements, such as axes, grooved and ungrooved, to which handles could be attached, chisels, gouges, occasional copper knives, flint blades, and scrapers.

They built houses, fences, palisades and platforms; they felled trees and peeled bark; they made canoes and dugouts, bows and arrow shafts, war clubs, hand spikes, digging tools, boat paddles, bowls, troughs, conductors, pails, tubs, spoons, and pot hooks; perhaps they used rollers, their nearest approach to wheels; and they made many other useful and necessary wooden contrivances. A man who does that kind of work we call a carpenter, and his tools may be called carpenters' tools.

Probably the barks of trees were of all woody material the easiest to procure and to form into shape. Indians did not make lumber. The words wigwam and tomahawk are constantly in popular use in speaking of Indians. Wigwam is virtually synonymous with the word house.

The more permanent and winter dwellings were dome-shaped. A skeleton of saplings was covered and closed in with large sheets of bark from such trees as birch, elm, cedar, basswood, etc. The Chippewas sometimes built, for temporary and summer use, conical wigwams like a tipi. Woven mats of cat-tails, rushes, and long grasses were also used for roofing and protection against the weather.

In some sections of the country, caves were occupied as habitations, but there were few cave dwellers here because there were very few caves. Upon Mackinac Island there should be evidences of old cave occupation.

It was a tedious and long process to fell a large tree and to dig it out for a boat. In such work, fire was employed, but the shaping and finishing was done with tools. Barks were fashioned into receptacles for storage and carrying. Canoes of bark were more common than dugouts. The birch bark canoe was so characteristic of the culture in the vicinity of the Great Lakes that occasionally one hears that region referred to as the birch bark area. From the inner fibrous strips of bark called 'bast,' cordage was made. Pieces of wood that were in constant use had to be freed from splinters and made smooth; for these purposes rubbing stones were used with sand and water. The use of sand for scouring and polishing purposes is very ancient. The sand and water process was largely employed in working down, grooving, boring, and polishing stone implements.

Clothing and Bodily Adornments. Clothing and bodily adornments were mostly made from animal skins. The hides of deer, because of their size and pliability, were extensively used in making large garments. Robes and mantles were made from beaver and other furs, being stitched together with sinew. Tanning was well developed so that the 'raw-hide' character of undressed skins was eliminated. Trappings were decorated in both curve and straight-line designs with porcupine quills, shells, and paints. Fringing about the ends of garments was produced by slitting the material. Breechcloth and leggins took the place of trousers. Moccasins with soft soles and drooping flaps protected the feet. Snow shoes were useful in winter travel. Women wore skirts which were made in one piece with the entire dress. Bear skins, buffalo robes, the skins of moose, elk, fox, wolf, otter, and the feather-bearing skins of birds contributed to comfort in cold weather. Coarse weaving and splint basketry were made by the women. Woven mats of flags and rushes covered both the floors and roofs of dwellings and served as screens and wind breaks.

Beads were an important part of the Indian's adornment. Many of the perforated stones, referred to elsewhere, were for ornament. Beads made of native and salt water shells, bone, copper, fossils, stone, teeth, ivory, claws, and in fact small hard objects of many materials through which a hole could be made, are found in abundance in old graves. These are so placed that we think they may have been upon strings and were buried with the decorations of the body. Beautiful fresh water pearls have been exhumed with skeletons in Ohio. Records of such beads from Michigan have not come to notice. Beads were worn as necklaces, belts, and arm and leg bands. They were also used as hair and head ornaments. Wampum has been mentioned under trade and commerce.

Aside from beads and other decorations, adornment was made of paints and greases. The Indian painted both himself and many of his accoutrements. In some localities he procured very good coloring matter from plant and berry juices. In graves, ocherous powders that were deposited at time of burial are frequently found. These mineral earths were probably used for cosmetics. Charcoal and soot made a good, if not a 'fast' black. Reds and yellows, mostly from ferruginous earthy materials, broke the somber monotony of his dusky complexion and added variation to the drabs and grays of his buckskin apparel. It is thought that some of the very small cupshaped mortars and diminutive pestles that are found were used for mixing pigments. Did the first American bring with him a fancy for decoration or was it acquired after he came to the New World?

In the ordinary fanciful pictures of Indians they are bedecked with feathers. There seems to have been a kind of code about the kind, number, and manner of wearing eagle, hawk, owl, goose, duck, and turkey feathers. They were to designate rank and prowess, when worn in certain ways. There was a prohibition against certain decorations upon the part of those who were not of sufficiently high rank or distinction to wear them in 'full dress.'

Runtees are usually of shell. The holes are drilled from edge to edge. In shape they are discoidal or circular and are very thin. Usually they are ornamented with star-shaped decorations. Parker[32] insinuates they are of Iroquoian origin and says: "Among the Algonkin tribes it is said that they were very highly valued." The only specimen we know of from this state, though no doubt there are many others, was collected in Wexford County in 1866. The material of this one appears to be ivory or bone. Runtees probably belong to the pendant class of objects and may have been worn as decorations as we use lockets and fobs. If one will trace the origin of ear rings, breast pins, brooches, belt buckles, hair ornaments, fringes, lockets, fobs, feather and fur ornamentation, bangles, and bows, he will find that savagery had them all and transmitted them to us. 'Taste' in

[32] The Archaeological History of New York. New York State Museum Bulletins, Nos. 235, 236, p. 434.

adornment has not materially changed with our civilization.

Medicine. The idea that diseases can be alleviated by 'treatment' is a very old one; certainly its origin goes down to a much lower stratum of culture than the American Indians' level. Medicine is a difficult term to define. The definitions of modern physicians set forth different conceptions from those the primitive people had of its scope. Medicine and religion were so mingled in the primitive mind that it was a long time before the fundamentals of each became separable. W. H. R. Rivers[33] says: "This continent affords a good example of the intimate relation between medicine and religion, the combination having developed to such an extent that most of the religious rites, rites often very elaborate and prolonged, have as their main purpose the treatment of sickness."

Prayer, song, ecstatic adoration, supplication, magic, legerdemain, sooth-saying, laying on of hands, fasting, feasting, massage, baths, sweats, physics, narcotics, fermented drinks, blood-letting, cupping, counter-irritants, poultices, salves, draughts, signs, suggestion, signatures, taboos, tonics, clysters, and blisters were all a part of the Indians' practices. Homeopathy with its 'similars,' Allopathy with its 'opposites,' Osteopathy with its 'manipulations,' Christian Science with its 'sittings.' Spiritualism with its 'seances,' are 'systems,' in their fundamentals, thousands of years older than is comprehended by most of those who practice them. Signs had to be right, rituals had to be performed, extra-human powers of both high and low degree had to be invoked, compensated, and propitiated. Particular spirits had to

[33] Medicine, Magic, and Religion, p. 73.

be called forth and malign ones had to be driven away. Sometimes the 'patient,' sometimes the doctor, sometimes some other person or thing had to 'take' the medicine or receive the treatment. One cannot describe the functions of doctors and priests separately. They were usually one and the same performer, employing both the ritual of religion and the practice of the medicine-man inseparably combined. There was no distinction between the two in the conception of the prehistoric invalid.

Cannibalism may have had its origin in 'medicine,' springing from the desire of the consumer to acquire the prowess, valor, and virtues of the consumed. In the conception of the savage, to partake of his body was the best way of partaking of the spirit of another person. Later this conception took on a more refined form and a vicarious substitute was used. On the theory that "a part strengthens a part," different organs and other parts of animals such as hearts, intestines, glands, brains, feet, and hands were eaten as medicine.

Whatever appeared to benefit or work to advantage, whether in curing or preventing disease or bringing good luck of any kind, was 'good medicine.'

The Indians had a wonderful pharmacy of plants and of "something to take in case of sickness." Edward Eggleston, in The Transit of Civilization, says that three hundred species of plants had been collected and were used as remedies by Indians.

Nothing about the Indians' methods and habits so much impressed the early settlers as their 'doctoring.' Charlatans and 'Indian Doctors' using 'hocus pocus' and swamp roots claimed to have been obtained from Indian mysteries, have thriven down to the present day.

It is a fact that from the botany of the New World several of our most valuable medicines have been obtained through the medium of Indians. Indians also had a rough-and-ready surgery and useful arts in the exigencies of forest life. Perhaps antidotes for snake bites and poisons have been exploited as much as any of the Indians' supposed specifics. Probably amulets, fetishes, gorgets, and a very large number of the so-called ceremonial and problematical relics were a part of the medicine men's armentaria.

The medicinal value of Peruvian Bark, of which quinine is an alkaloid, was learned from the natives in South America by Jesuit missionaries. Ipecac, at one time so much used in medical practice, was also used by the natives of tropical South America. Coco, which yields cocain, was the divine plant of the Incas. Tobacco was 'great medicine.' Sarsaparilla is also from tropical America. Boneset, golden seal, snakeroot, ginseng, lady's slipper, ivy, wild cherry, prickly ash, jimson-weed, are among the plants common in Michigan that are claimed to have 'medicinal properties.'

There was among the Chippewa and neighboring tribes a secret medicine society or lodge, the Midewiwin, that had four degrees. This 'ancient order' had great influence and as one advanced through the degrees his ability to cure disease and his spiritual insight and powers successively increased.

Perforation of Skulls. Years ago, a very important mound discovery was made, as narrated by Mr. Henry Gillman,[34] in what was called the Great Mound of the Rouge River near Detroit. A number of human skulls that were taken from the mound had been artificially perforated. The apertures varied from less than a half-

[34] Certain Characteristics Pertaining to Ancient Man in Michigan. Smithsonian Report, 1875, p. 234.

inch to nearly an inch across. They were round with somewhat flaring edges, some giving evidence of having been bored with a stone point or a flint 'drill'. Similar specimens were found elsewhere in the eastern part of the state in the Lake Huron drainage. Mr. Gillman states that the perforations were made after death. There is in the University Museum a specimen of real trephining, from near Devil River Mound. A very symmetrical hole was bored in the top of the skull while the person was still alive. The edges of the opening show unmistakable evidence of a well-advanced healing process which could have gone on only during life.

Trephined skulls have been found in places far distant from here, being very numerous in Peru and in Mexico. From nowhere, however, in the Great Lakes Region have many, if any, been reported except from Michigan. One might ask why the skulls were perforated. In the majority of specimens the operation was probably performed after or immediately preceding death. Mr. Hrdlička suggests that the skulls bored after death were so treated for the purpose of securing the 'button' as a fetish. Some of the heads might have been 'operated upon' with a view of removing pieces of weapons or for restoring the shape of the head after a severe thump. The skull in the Museum, to which reference has been made, shows no evidence of either injury or disease. In the Michigan specimens, the perforations are usually directly in the center of the vertex. The operation may have been performed for some medico-religious reason; to let a bad spirit out or a good one in; either of which, of course, is a wild conjecture. The fact remains that perfectly normal skulls were trephined while the subject was alive.

Professor Roy S. Moodie[35] asserts with great assurance that ancient trephining was for the relief of headache. It is surprising to note in the Hand Book of American Indians, under 'Medicine and Medicine Men,' the statement—''trephining has never been found north of Mexico.'' We may safely say that trephining, though not extensively practiced, was a distinctive trait of Michigan culture. Of itself, it constitutes a topic well worth intensive study.

It is common to find pieces of pottery with holes broken through the bottom. While the pots were not damaged in any other way they were purposely punctured, probably at the time of being placed in graves. Such specimens are said to be 'killed', that is, they were broken through so as to release the spirits they contained. Besides killing pottery, the custom was, in some districts, to kill weapons, pipes, and other entombed articles. This may account for finding so many broken specimens in graves and mounds. The killing set free the spirits of the objects so they could readily take flight with the spirit of the dead person. Is it not possible that the same animistic conception that led to the killing of pottery, weapons, etc., was also a reason for perforating human skulls? The killing would, according to an Indian's conception, enable a quicker release of the spirit.

Caches or Hoards. Numbers of artifacts of the same type are frequently found in a cluster or deposit together. Such deposits are called by American archaeologists, caches, by the English, hoards. The use of the word cache is confusing because sometimes it is made

[35] Scientific Monthly, Feb., 1921, p. 161.

to refer to the place of storage, sometimes to the things stored. Oftentimes the circumstances indicate that articles were hidden against theft. In the mound region, unfinished implements of flint are found hoarded in large numbers. These are usually leaf-shaped and are called blanks. The intent may have been to store them until they could be reduced to the desired shape at the convenience of the owner. No doubt articles were hidden in caches while journeys were taken.

Some immense deposits of flint flakes are reported from different places. One conjecture is that the articles were sometimes votive, or ceremoniously buried as accoutrements of the dead. ''It is probable that many of these caches of flaked stones are accumulations of incipient implements roughed out at the quarries and carried away for further specialization and use.''

In this state, caches of copper implements and nuggets are occasionally reported. They are found hidden among large boulders, under stumps of trees, in mounds, graves and gravel banks—so isolated, at times, that they must have been secreted for the sake of safety. The Indian had the fundamental idea of the modern 'safety deposit drawer' for rental at every bank to-day.

Domestic Life. In the popular conception all Indians were very much alike and when one individual or group is described the description answers for all. Many judge Indian life from what they may have seen or heard about the Plains People, whose nomadic careers but recently came to a close. On the contrary, as has been explained elsewhere, there was a great difference in customs, springing, for one reason, from different environments.

The attempt in this volume, vague as descriptions may be, is to restore some of the settings of the forest-dwellers of Michigan which were as distinct from some of the other Indians as the woods were different from the prairies. The daily routine was, of course, sombre and monotonous but the division of labor between the sexes was as clearly cut as is our own. The man was a hunter and a warrior. When not upon the 'path' he was upon the 'chase', and the women, largely, had to fend for themselves. The hunters brought the game. The women dressed it and converted it into a part of the supply of provisions. Among those tribes which raised corn, the women cleared the ground, planted, harvested, and made the hominy and meal cakes, although as they had 'off hours' the men helped in producing the crop. On moving day, if the canoe could not be used, the women were the burden bearers carrying the lodge coverings. The man had to be free from hindrance because at any moment, in time of war, he must be untrammeled and alert to defend his weaklings against attack, besides, upon him devolved the necessity of killing deer, wild turkeys and other game for the night's and morning's meals. The women gathered the wood, kept the fire, brought the water, stewed, roasted and baked. They made baskets and bark containers. The Indian woman made excellent pails from bark by folding the corners and securing them with binders. In sugar making, she furnished the utensils and did the work. Baskets, bark boxes, hampers and bags took the place of trunks, satchels, bureaus and cupboards. She wove mats and did exceedingly creditable 'fancy work' with quills, feathers and hair. She was the tanner and potter. She and her children collected berries, nuts, roots, herbs, and shell fish. Her poultry yard consisted of the wild turkeys, water fowls and other birds which contributed eggs, however stealthily they may have secreted their nests. Wooden utensils, hunting gear, traps, weapons of warfare, and stone and flint work came within the province of the men's work. As in modern society, the men were usually away on the business of providing supplies and keeping up the 'improvements' and defences of the community. The women were at the hearth converting supplies into victuals, adding what they could from gleanings.

The children, like the fawns and cubs of the wild, disported themselves, abiding the time when the burdens of self-support should devolve upon them. The family government was by suasion and example rather than by fear and punishment. The adolescents were gradually brought under rather strict discipline to prepare them in the rituals of conduct and ways of the woods and the lakes. The aged were in the way as soon as they became unable to assist the women and children in the village drudgery and probably were so severely dealt with, when they could not keep up with the march, as to cause their elimination. They were sometimes left behind on the march to fall prey to predatory animals. Once in a while a wise old crone or a cunning old man would be pampered and their lives made comfortable to the last moment on account of their 'medicine.'

Rock Carvings and Drawings. Rock carvings and drawings are not much in evidence in this state. On the north branch of Cass River in Greenleaf Township, Sanilac County, are some crude carvings of men, animals and birds. It is doubted whether they are of genuine Indian work. If not, whoever made them was no doubt familiar with carvings in Ontario, Canada, which they endeavored to imitate.

There are some red paintings on limestone at the entrance to a cave at Burnt Bluff near Fayette in the Upper Peninsula that appear to be genuine Indian types, if not of genuine Indian execution.

CHAPTER VIII

CLASSIFICATION AND DESCRIPTION OF ARTIFACTS

Whoever has given attention to the relics of Indian make is familiar with a general classification. The pattern that is employed by Old World archaeologists does not fit in America. The classical divisions, eolithic, palaeolithic, neolithic, bronze, and iron, must be disregarded in dealing with New World culture. In Europe, stratifications are so clearly distinguishable that the palaeolithic period is subdivided into two general and several minor classes. Speaking loosely, a palaeolithic specimen is roughly made without finishing touches and is not polished; a neolithic specimen is one that has been polished and carefully worked into shape. According to that description, our fields were strewn with both kinds. Thousands of exceedingly rough tools were found; also, large numbers that are wrought with great refinement in conception and finish are picked up. Technically, the two periods, the Old Stone Age and the New Stone Age, consisted in types of general culture of which implements are but a part. The terms apply to culture grades, not merely to the handiwork of a tool maker. If we use any term of European classification in connection with Indian artifacts it should be 'neolithic,' that is, the culture of a late Stone Period to which the common Indians belonged.

One who undertakes to describe the material as well as the manner of making and the uses of numerous finds attributed to the Indians, has quite a technical task. Mr. W. K. Moorehead's book, "The Stone Age in America," is probably the best reference. In the Report of the National Museum, 1897, Thomas Wilson has nearly two hundred pages upon arrows, spearheads and knives of pre-historic times: a description which is quite exhaustive. Reports of the Bureau of Ethnology, Smithsonian Reports, The Handbook of American Indians, and many other books upon primitive industry describe and classify artifacts so well that all there is needed in this connection is to speak briefly of types that have been found in Michigan. No doubt many will be overlooked.

Flints; Arrows, Spears, Scrapers, Drills, Knives, etc. The material that was used in making implements that pass under the names is usually called flint. It requires the expert opinion of a trained mineralogist to classify flinty stones. Sometimes he will wish to make laboratory tests to determine accurately their composition. He will speak of chalcedony, jasper, quartzite, obsidian, horn-stone, chert, and other silicious stones, but flint will serve our purpose as a blanket term.

A pointed, thin, flint implement under two inches in length, with two sharp edges, is usually described as an arrow point. One that is of the same general appearance and form but over that length is called a spear, but the distinction is purely arbitrary. What distinction the Indians made, we cannot say. Arrow points were attached to shafts for shooting from bows. Spears may also have been used in that way but the longer and heavier ones certainly would have been useless for projectile points. That they were really attached to handles or 'stales' like a pitchfork, we do not know, nor is it clear of what great use they would have been. Many of them are too dull or rough to be of use in perforating the skins and flesh of animals or men. Skin and thick muscle are not much more easily punctured than India rubber. 'To get through,' a sharp, tapering point driven with great velocity would be necessary, although a vigorous thrust could drive 'home' a pointed cutting edge. While so-called Indian spears look formidable, if one stops to contemplate he will be more or less skeptical as to whether they were intended for actual use in combat or in the chase. A sharpened shaft of dried, seasoned hickory, iron-wood, ash, or other tough wood would have gotten through the integument of an adversary more easily than any large flint spear-head. We certainly describe many specimens as spears for want of a better term. As cited elsewhere, Wissler says that no lances were used by the eastern woodland Indians.

Over forty distinct forms of arrows and flints are ascribed to the Algonquians and probably all of them are identified with Michigan workmanship. The largest spear from the state of which we definitely know belongs to Mr. Jay See of Diamondale. It is not made of flint but is perfectly chipped with barbs and neck; the length is twelve and one half inches; the width five and three quarters inches. It was probably a digging tool. Mr. Henry Gilman[36] reports: "Lances or spear-heads of remarkable length, two of them being a foot long, and one sixteen inches in length." These he secured in a mound upon Black River, St. Clair County. Flint specimens of all patterns are picked up upon the surface, found in burial places, upon village

[36] Annual Report Smithsonian Institution, 1873, p. 373.

sites, in fact almost anywhere. It is said of Thoreau: "Once, when out walking, a friend asked him where Indian arrow heads could be found. 'Everywhere,' was his reply, and, stooping down, picked one up.''

No doubt a large number of chipped points and blades, varying in excellency of workmanship, were cutting tools or knives. Perhaps many of the so-called spears were knives. Some were probably digging tools. The edge would decide the usefulness of a tool for cutting. Flint knives are thinner than most of the notched or square-based spears. Some knives are oval, some lanciform, some double-edged. The best of them are made of better material than ordinary arrow points. Some probably had handles attached, others were used without hafts. Many specimens designated as knives were very effective; others require a considerable stretching of the imagination to make out how they could have been used for cutting. Knives were used in symbolism. Once in a while a knife appears that crudely resembles a spoke-shave. 'Razor blades' are long, thin, flint flakes with a keen edge following the line of fracture.

Knife-like tools were made of shell, bone, antler, teeth, wood, and of any other available material that would take an edge. A large number of blunt pieces, appearing to be broken arrows or spears rounded off, are called scrapers. Some are referred to as 'bunts.' Scrapers could be used for clearing the bark from wood, or the flesh and periostium from bones, as well as hollowing out cavities. It is an interesting, if not useful, play of the imagination to consider what one would do if placed in the Indian's situation, having nothing to work with but the same contrivances which he had. The inventive faculty would certainly be stimulated to produce adaptations and improved tools.

Drills are represented in nearly every collection of flint implements. They are commonly formed like a pencil with a flaring head. We have heard them called Indian scratch awls. Usually they are brought to a boring point so that they could have been used in drilling holes through shale, shell, pottery fragments, and that general class of perforated trinkets called gorgets, pendants, etc. The effect is like a countersink. Occasionally there is a drill which is a wonderful specimen of workmanship; long, slender, circular in cross section, and artistic. Such ones could be used in deep drilling, as in boring pipes, stems, tubes, and banner-stones, but a few of them appear to be too exquisitely chipped down to have been used for any risky purpose. Boring was done with contrivances other than flint drills. With patience and skill, a hole can be bored into a hard stone with a hollow reed stalk, like a wild sunflower stem, by means of a rotary motion, using sand and water. Many long tubes, pipes, and other hollow artifacts were probably worked out with some such machine: the forerunner of the diamond drill. A machine is a contrivance working in more than one piece to produce a certain effect upon material. A fire-drill, a boring apparatus, bows and arrows are all machines. Knives, pestles, scrapers, clubs, etc., are tools.

Many specialized designs in flint, such as the so-called saws, disks, hoes, spades, 'effigies' and even human profiles, are found. It seems that flint chipping with the Indian, like the Yankee's whittling, was a pastime. If the writer were to have every type of chipped flint presented to him for classification, the miscellaneous and problematical group would contain more forms than all the others combined.

Axes, Celts, Hammers, etc. The nomenclature of the axe group of tools is somewhat mixed. Usually the term 'Indian axe' refers to those edged tools of stone that have grooves either completely or partially surrounding the head at the poll. Those without a groove are by some called celts, by others hatchets, ungrooved axes, tomahawks, skinning stones, fleshers, etc. If one is flat upon one side, it is an adze. If it is hollowed, so that the edge is a segment of a circle, it is a gouge. If it is blunt with a groove, it is a maul. If it is ovoid in outline with a depression upon one or both sides it is, by some, called a 'thumb and finger stone,' by others a hand hammer, a pounder, etc. Sometimes mauls appear to have been made-over broken axes.

The grooving of axes is interesting. Upon some the groove encircles the entire head; with others the groove is upon only the wide faces; others have the handle groove upon the two wide and only one of the narrow faces; once in a while one has a longitudinal groove upon one narrow face as if to receive a wedge for tightening the handle. Upon some specimens the groove goes diagonally across the upper part of the axe. Schoolcraft[37] gives the following description of such an axe: "The mode of using this ancient axe, which would be more appropriately classed as a pick, was by twisting around it, of a size corresponding to the ring, a supple withe, forming a handle, which could be firmly tied together, and which would enable the user to strike a firm inward blow. The handle was not at right angles with the axe. It was placed, as the ring shows, so that at about the length of three feet it would intersect a line drawn at

[37] Historical and Statistical Information, Part I, p. 76.

right angles from the foot of the blade, or edge of great-est sharpness. This incidence of handle to the blade would enable an indrawing blow to be struck, which there are practical reasons for.''

A rare type of axe with flutings has been found upon both sides of Lake Michigan; more in Wisconsin than in Michigan. They are generally well made, indicating that much time was spent in working them down. They are mostly grooved like the common axe with flutings running longitudinally. A few, however, are fluted transversely. Double-bitted and double-grooved axes are rare in this state; there are a few in the hands of private collectors. There is a type of axe with a very wide groove and raised knobs upon the narrow sides called 'the Michigan axe.' Upon some of these axes the groove is three inches wide. If one will exercise a little imagina-tion he will discern that this type may be referred to as 'effigy axes.' The writer ventures to describe them by that term. Occasionally an axe is of unwieldy size, weighing nearly twenty pounds, others are as small as two or three inches in length. We always associate axes and hatchets with the act of chopping. It is a question whether all axes were for the purpose that their appearance suggests. The same may be said of other types of artifacts, which belong to the 'problematical' class. Celts, or axe-like tools without grooves, are an interesting group, varying in type and workmanship in marked degree. Their variation in size is as great as that of axes.

A good many very well made gouges and adzes are found in the state. Mauls and pounders, both with and without grooves, of immense weight occur in the copper mining country. Considering their weight, some of them could not have been used by one man. Others are so small and neat as to be mere Indian 'tack hammers.' The material of which this general class of implements is made is a hard, granite-like stone that escaped the pulverizing influence of glacial grinding and flood wash. Some celts are so thin and well edged as to be called chisels. Others may, perhaps, have been wedges. Copper was worked into axes, hatchets, and chisels. Copper mauls weighing over twenty pounds are reported from the old mines upon the Ontonagon. Copper gads and chisels have also been reclaimed from the mining pits. As with other classes of artifacts, an occasional specimen is so well fashioned and polished, so symmetrical and exquisite, one may infer it was not for ordinary use but for formal and ritualistic purposes and belonged to some distinguished person or group.

Ceremonials.   There are found pretty well scattered over the state objects called gorgets, banner stones, birdstones, pendants, amulets, etc. They are usually classified as ceremonials or problematical objects and are not often found in graves or in mounds. Wissler suggests that they may be older than mound culture. It is a fact, however, that the distribution of these pieces, usually made of slate, corresponds quite closely throughout the country with the distribution of the linguistic family called Algonquian.

The average collector, obsessed with the idea that pretty objects are more valuable, specializes in ceremonials. On account of their being made usually of slaty stone, they are by some called slates, just as we designate another group of artifacts by the generic term flints. One must not lose sight of the fact that the aim in collecting relics, digging into mounds, clearing out

pit-holes, searching over camp-sites, and of other archaeological investigation is to trace resemblances and to note
differences among them with a view of determining cultural lines and not to assemble bric-a-brac and curios.

The writer once asked a country boy if he knew of
any Indian relics. He said, "Yes, I've got a little
sheep." The little sheep turned out to be a bird-stone.
The bird-stones are well designated because usually they
resemble birds in shape, although, as was the case with
the boy, other animal forms are discerned. Some approach the turtle shape. They are distributed over the
territory of Algonquian occupation and are probably
more common in this than in any other state. One of
the archaeological puzzles is to ascribe some use to these
effigies. One man's guess is likely to be as good as another's in this riddle. Mr. A. C. Parker, in the Archaeological History of New York, Part 1, after saying there
is no known use for them suggests no less than seven
possible purposes to which they might have been put.

Certain forms of bird-stones have knob-like projec-
tions from the head, resembling eyes. Occasionally one
has perforations through the head for eyes. Other forms
are not so elaborate. There appears to be a gradation
from the common bar amulet up to specimens with high
heads, flaring tails, long necks, wings, etc. They are
not all made of slate. Very hard and mottled igneous
stone was occasionally worked, evidently with much
patience and endless labor, into bird-like forms. One
fact is worthy of mention: nearly all bird-stones have
perforations at the base; from this it may be concluded
that they were attached to some other object. If one
were going to classify bird-stones he would have as many
classes as there are specimens because there are scarcely

two alike. Moorehead gives a chart of slate designs. We counted up to a hundred and decided that the conclusion just expressed was the correct one.

Slate, usually banded pieces being selected, was made into crescent-shaped objects. Sometimes the crescents are double, presenting an appearance of having four horns. A single crescent, on account of its shape, is described as a crutch-stone. Banner stones resembling light, double-bitted hatchets are not so much elaborated as 'butterflies.' Some slates are pointed and straight like a pick. Others have square blades. There is an uncountable variety of the fanciful slate trinkets and ornaments that are found in collections. As intimated elsewhere, they may belong to an older culture than that of the tribes that are known to us by their historical names.

A good many egg-shaped specimens are found with creases or shallow grooves about the smaller end, but some are perforated. This type is called, by collectors, plummets or sinkers. Sinkers are often roughly made, being nothing more than small stones with a slight groove about them. The groove was presumably for attaching a string. They may very properly be described as net sinkers although there is a theory that some were used as weights in weaving.

Long smooth and finely-bored stone tubes, usually of slate, are not uncommon. Some of them are nearly a foot long, accurately bored and elegantly shaped. If the tube is funnel-shaped in the bore, it is probably a tubular pipe. The holes through some specimens are not circular in cross section, but elliptical, presenting a complicated method of boring.

Butterfly stones are much like banner stones but are cut down at the base of the blades or wings, which are usually pointed. Like all the other drilled fanciful forms, it seems impossible to determine their use. They make a fine display in a collection as well as attractive illustrative material for books. They, together with the other objects found with them, may help to solve the problem of culture areas.

Clubs. Clubs were among the first, if they were not the first, tools and weapons used by savage man. In the beginning he satisfied himself with any common cudgel, but as he improved in workmanship, clubs took symmetrical shapes, with the center of balance near the head.

Several tribes could be identified by the form and decorations of their clubs, which were mounted with stone, bones, and antler points to make them more effective. Scepters, truncheons, maces and batons, all emblems of authority, are clubs so refined in form and beauty that they have become purely emblematical.

In speaking of the development of the mace from the knotty clubs of early man, Balfour[38] makes the following comment: ''Clubs such as these were the forerunners of the terrible iron maces with which our scrupulous militant bishops formerly armed themselves in preference to swords, on the plea that they were not calculated to shed blood. A truly delightful piece of sophistry!''

It is very probable that butterfly stones, banner stones, and perforated blades, too fragile for any use, were borne by select men among the Indians as emblems of authority. If so, when placed upon handles, they showed an extreme specialization, the stages of develop-

[38] The Evolution of Decorative Art, p. 95.

ment being cudgel, ornamented club, mace, baton, scepter, etc. The 'battle axe,' like the modern military man's dress sword, also became a purely decorative ceremonial signifying rank and distinction.

Gorgets. Gorgets are the most varied and numerous forms of perforated stones. Sometimes blanks, flat, thin, smooth pieces of slate without holes through them, appear. The drill-holes through gorgets vary in number from one to five or six, but two is the usual number. The drillings usually appear to have been from both sides and do not always 'jibe' perfectly in the center, showing that the makers were not very exact in measuring. Those that have been drilled from both sides show an effect much like countersinking, although through some the perforations are clear cut and of the same calibre all the way through.

Slate was generally used in making this kind of object, but harder and finely mottled stones were polished down and drilled. A considerable number of shell gorgets which are etched upon one or both faces are reported. The length of gorgets seldom exceeds six or eight inches; in width they are from four inches down to narrow strips. Two or three inches is the usual width. They are seldom as thick as half an inch. They are of innumerable shapes: the parallelogram is the commonest outline; others are elliptical, triangular, spatulate, shield-shaped, constricted, and notched. Those that have fine nicks around the edge are called tally stones. 'Tally marks' are also common upon many kinds of objects. They were probably notched in, not as tallies, but for embellishment.

With the exception of pipes and tubes, it would seem that all pieces of whatever description with holes through them were to be attached with strings or placed upon sticks. Not many of them, however, show friction marks as would appear after much wear. We have heard these objects called shuttles, sighting stones, belt buckles, buttons, hair ornaments, etc. They are of so many shapes, however, that there are not guesses enough to go around. They are found so placed in graves that they appear to have been attached to the wrists.

These objects have been called gorgets because they were conjectured to have been worn at the throat or gorge.

Pipes and Smoking.   Pipes overlap or interblend with nearly all culture areas; however, each area had pipe forms that were more or less peculiar to it. Pipes in grotesque shapes are found and may be ascribed, perhaps, to totemistic expressions. Turtles, birds, amphibians, serpents, various other animals, human faces and heads, parts of the bodies of people and animals, fishes, flowers, gods and devils, would all seem to have been taken as models in pipe making. Others are very plain and without any ornament.

Of the thousands of pipes that have been reclaimed from graves, sites, mounds, and elsewhere there are hardly two alike. Each one has an individuality. Many are high expressions of Indian art. A few are heavy, weighing two or more pounds. The present day smoker would say that such pipes are not 'practical' because he could not place the stem in his mouth and walk off. To smoke a tube pipe one must have been obliged to be in a reclining attitude. For heavy pipes, when in use, some support was probably used. Once in a while a pipe is found with two, or even more, stemholes. We have heard these called bridegroom pipes and council pipes. Pipes were made of almost all the different materials known to Indian workmanship. Many varieties of workable stone, wood, clay, and even copper were wrought into pipes.

Pottery pipes are exceedingly common throughout Michigan, Canada, New York, and New England. Beautiful shapes were made of Huronic slate. In the mound area, especially south of Michigan, the platform or 'monitor' form is common among pipes. These are very rare north of Ohio. Probably a large number of pipes classify as 'ceremonials,' and in this one instance we know pretty well the part they played in the ceremony.

The Indian used tobacco as a sacred or specific substance to be smoked in formality. In ceremony the 'emblems' are generally elaborately decorated. We, too, have beautiful tankards, chalices, beakers, communion services and fonts, but our conception in those things is not new.

In councils, conferences, treaties, at the opening of the hunting and fishing seasons, upon adventures in war, at dances, in invoking the powers for whatever purpose, magic, witchcraft, curing disease, help or guidance, smoking was a dignified and necessary part of the ritual. Among the last things an Indian would part with was his sacred pipe.

How far Indians indulged in the smoking habit apart from etiquette and formal functions is not definitely known, but probably not so much as we do who smoke from habit only. Cigarettes and cigars are said to have been made by some Indians but probably not by those living in this region.

Otis T. Mason describes the process of making pipe stems along the Great Lakes. A stick was split from end to end. The half cavities were gouged out from the interior of each piece and then the pieces were united by means of a gum or glue and lashed when wet. After shrinking, the whole was as solid as ever. In passing, it might be mentioned that many primitive people were expert makers and users of sticking material. Points were fixed in arrow shafts, handles made rigid to their attachments and splices were united by gluing. In the same way, withes were reinforced and cords prevented from loosening. Excellent glues could have been made then, the same as now, from parts of fish, the hoofs and cartilages of animals, the young sprouts of deer's horns, resins, gums, etc.

The Indian used other smoke-making material than tobacco. He made 'blends' from the barks of willow, dogwoods, sumac and the leaves of certain plants. Kinnikinnick, a Chippewa word which means 'hand-mixed,' was sometimes used to describe smoking mixtures.

Mortars and Pestles. Mortars and pestles are common. The mortars from this state that are made of stone are mostly quite shallow. They are not generally reduced to symmetrical form upon the outside, as are many fine ones from the Pacific slope. Hollowed out log-ends were used with long pestles for reducing grain, nuts, seeds, and probably dried flesh to powder. Some very fine roller pestles have been collected in the state. Roller pestles are sometimes of so much weight that, as Schoolcraft suggests, they were probably worked with a spring pole. A few are so perfectly cylindrical that they could have been used as 'rolling pins' upon a smooth surface. The bell-shaped pestle is common.

Pottery. It is almost impossible to think of living without 'dishes.' The first spoons may have been clam shells. Large shells, turtles' carapaces, skulls, buffalo horns, gourds and other hollow objects were used for dippers. Man had to have some means for carrying water before he could cook by boiling. Cooking containers were made of hides of animals held in hollows in the ground, or by some support, the heat being applied by dropping hot stones into them. The western Indians made cooking baskets.

Pottery making was a well advanced art of the Michigan Indians. Vessels of pottery served admirably for kettles, cups, and other culinary purposes. They varied in size and shape and were moulded by the fingers of the potter, probably a woman.

A pot that held eight gallons is reported from Washtenaw County, another from Macomb County had a capacity of fifteen gallons. Those of such large size must have been difficult to keep in shape until baked and after that required care in handling. Models of pottery varied, apparently, as much among the savage as among civilized makers. Clay is an ideal material for the expression of fancy and imagery.

The hardening of pottery was probably not done in an oven or kiln, but by the open hearth. After the pieces were dried by atmospheric exposure they were baked by piling combustible material around them which was set on fire. The heat of fire and ashes rendered the pots firm and impervious to water. Wandering tribes, continually changing places of abode, could not have made nor used much pottery on account of its liability to breakage in transporting. The making and use of pottery, like corn growing, indicates a more or less sedentary habit of the makers and growers.

Pottery, even in fragments, may give a clue to the tribe of makers, as each left its peculiar distinguishing marks in shape and decoration upon their wares. Algonquian and Iroquois pots are usually readily distinguished.

It would be very instructive to locate the old potteries because clays and other ingredients that went into the paste are local in their distribution. There is a clay or slush bed, reported by Mr. P. S. Lovejoy, in Klacking Township, Ogemaw County, where the Indians are supposed to have made pottery. Another ancient pottery was located upon Grand River below Grand Rapids. If one were to look for them in clay districts other potteries would be found. Mr. Henry Gilman was inclined to think there must have been a place where the manufacture of pottery was carried on to an unusual extent at the head of Lake St. Clair.

If all the pottery that has been unearthed in Michigan, and there would be hundreds of whole pieces, saying nothing of fragments, were assembled into one collection, an archaeologist who has made a study of American ceramics could translate them into terms of tribal distributions.

From the mounds in Springwells Township, Wayne County, were removed some unusually fine specimens of whole pottery which Mr. Gilman many years ago placed in the Archaeological Museum, Cambridge, Massachusetts. If one wishes to study Michigan pottery he will have to go to museums outside of the state to find the most of the specimens. The Museum of the University of Michigan does not possess a single entire piece of Michigan pottery although it has representative specimens from South America, Panama and Florida. Kent Scientific Museum, in Grand Rapids, has a number of fine specimens from mounds in that locality. There are a few other specimens in private local collections.

Pottery or clay pipes are numerous throughout the state. They are observed to increase in frequency as one advances northward from the southern boundary. The majority of them are clumsy, heavy, and lack the finish of the stone pipes common in the southern tiers of counties. There are observed various types of these pipes. Many have flattened stems, and with others the stem is the heaviest part. The majority of them have quite sharp elbows. If they could all be assembled and arranged into series with respect to pattern and local distribution, interesting deductions could be made from them. It must be borne in mind that trade pipes are easily confused with real Indian types.

Copper. Copper and other minerals, if used at all, had to be mined where nature placed them; whereas earthworks could be located almost anywhere at the caprice of the builders. If the copper deposits had been in some other territory, mining could not have been a part of our primitive industry. It is a question whether securing metal from the seams and crevices of rocks was a specialty of a group of local miners or whether Indians from different and remote settlements did not come to the copper ranges, secure their supply and return home, just as a band would go long distances upon hunting excursions and return after securing their game. The same question might be asked about the flint quarries of other states and the mica beds of the Carolinas. Were there a number of operators who worked at procuring these several minerals as a trade?

A large quantity of the copper used by the Indians in their art was 'float' copper. Pieces of it had been carried by ice and deposited in the drift as far south as the mouth of the Ohio River. The nearer one approached the original deposits the more numerous would be the float pieces. Thousands of such detached fragments were found not far from the mines, and were distributed by the finders to distant parts just as were the pieces wrested from the seams of the rocks. There may have been cults of copper 'finders' or hunters as there may have been miners.

Anyone interested in the Ancient Mining on the Shores of Lake Superior should peruse a report by that title written by Charles Whittlesey, Smithsonian Contribution to Science, Vol. XIII. No facts of importance have been added to the subject since Mr. Whittlesey, a trained geologist and archaeologist, made his original lucid report. A number of papers upon the subject are to be found in various volumes of the Michigan Pioneer and Historical Collections, all drawing largely upon what Whittlesey said. Whittlesey's report, which is not easily obtainable at present, should be re-published. It is well illustrated and was made before modern industries had disturbed the situation as the Indians left it.

According to Mr. Charles T. Jackson, U. S. Geological Surveyor, 1849, the Indians were wary about imparting information concerning localities of copper and about giving up any pieces of the metal in their possession. Jackson states:[39] "It is not surprising that the Indian priests should have exerted themselves to gain control of the native copper mines, and that they should have endeavored to monopolize the exorcising of the Evil Manitou, who was supposed to be intrusted with the guardianship of this valuable metal, but that they should impress on the superstitious minds of the Indians the necessity of keeping the valuable localities a profound

[39] Geological and Mineralogical Reports. Executive Doc. No. 1, U. S. Senate, 31st Congress, Dec. 24, 1849, p. 375.

secret from all strangers, warning them that they would die if they revealed them. This superstition the ancient Jesuit Fathers found to be universal among the Chippewas two hundred years ago.''

Another of the conspicuous needs in the field of Michigan archaeology is an exhaustive scientific survey of Keweenaw Peninsula and Isle Royale to determine more definitely the history of the ancient mines and 'workings' of copper. There is an instructive account of a survey of the ancient mines upon Isle Royale by Mr. W. H. Holmes (American Anthropologist, Vol. III, No. 4).

Whether or not the occupation of securing native copper from natural deposits was a specialized occupation of particular men, it can hardly be denied that the fashioning of the copper, rough from the ground, into implements and ornaments was so much of an art that one may say there were coppersmiths among the Indians. Considering the tools they worked with and that the Indians in the Great Lakes district did not know how to smelt, braze, or weld, their work as gathered by collectors shows a degree of skill in manipulating copper comparable with that of white hand-workmen.

If one wishes to start a controversy with the usual collector of copper implements, let him challenge the statement that the Indians tempered copper. Metallurgists say copper cannot be tempered. A good many copper knives have quite sharp edges but hardly keen enough for cutting soft wood effectively without great effort. The writer once heard a man declare that the edges of the tempered copper knives he had were as hard as steel and he could shave with them, but when a 'fee' was offered to see the shaving done, there was no warm water.

There is no positive evidence that the Indian copper-smiths used heat in bringing the metal into shape. The shaping appears to have been done cold, mostly by pounding and bending. As the native metal was hammered it took on a firm edge and a harder character. Sharp edges were probably produced by means of gritty stones used as whetstones. Thousands of copper objects such as knives, arrow and spear points, hatchets, axes, hammers, chisels, pins, needles, awls, pendants and other ornaments, tubes, beads, and even pipes, have been collected in various parts of the state. Tons of similar things have been gathered within a thousand miles of the Lake Superior region.

Some remarkable nuggets of crude metal have been taken from mounds. The following extract from History of the City of Grand Rapids, by Gilbert Baxter, 1891, referring to finds made by Mr. W. L. Coffinberry, who made explorations in the Grand River district and reported extensively upon the archaeology of that region, is interesting in this connection: ''In the City of Grand Rapids there were mounds—Beneath the base of a mound in Court Street were taken two nuggets of native silver (about 13 pounds) and one of copper (about 14 pounds), etc., which Mr. Coffinberry sold to the Curator of Peabody Museum, Salem, Mass., for $200.'' Manuscripts of Mr. Coffinberry in the library of the Kent Scientific Institute also refer to this find and photographs of the nuggets are attached to the descriptions.

If one were to mention the outstanding peculiarities of prehistoric Michigan he would say the garden beds and the copper mines were the most conspicuous. The garden beds are destroyed, but the old mining pits may yet be studied, especially upon Isle Royale, and should be protected against unintelligent despoliation.

CHAPTER IX

REFERENCES - HINSDALE

Annual Reports of the Smithsonian Institution.

Archaeological Reports of Ontario.

BLOIS, JOHN T. Gazetteer of the State of Michigan. Sydney L. Rood and Co., Detroit, 1838.

Bureau of American Ethnology Publications.

BUSHNELL, DAVIL I., JR. Native Villages and Village Sites East of the Mississippi. Bureau of Ethnology, Bulletin 69, Smithsonian Institution, Washington, 1919.

COLDEN, CADWALLADER. The History of the Five Nations of Canada. Third Edition, London, 1755.

COOK, DARIUS B. Six Months Among the Indians. Niles Mirror Office, Niles, Mich., 1889.

CRAWFORD, O.S.G. Man and His Past. Oxford University Press, 1921.

DELLENBAUGH, FREDERICK S. The North Americans of Yesterday. G.P. Putnam's Sons, New York, 1901.

FOWKE, GERARD. Archaeological History of Ohio. Ohio State Archaeological and Historical Society Columbus, 1902.

FOX, GEORGE R. What about Michigan Archaeology? Michigan History Magazine, Vol. VI, 1922.

Handbook of American Indians. Bureau of Ethnology, Smithsonian Institution, Washington, 1912.

HUBBARD, BELA. Memorials of a Half-Century. G.P. Putnam's Sons, New York and London, 1887.

HUDSON, W.H. The Book of a Naturalist. Geo. H. Doran, New York, 1919.

KROEBER. A.L. Anthropology. Harcourt Brace and Co., n.d. Local and County Histories.

LOWIE, ROBERT H. Primitive Society. Boni Liveright, New York, 1920.

MACALISTER, R.A.S. Textbook of European Archaeology. Cambridge University Press, London, 1921.

MACCULLOCH, JAMES A. The Childhood of Fiction. E.P. Dutton and Co., New York, 1905.

MARETT, R.R. Anthropology. Henry Holt and Co., New York, n.d.

MASON, OTIS T. The Origin of Invention. Charles Scribner's Sons, New York.

Jesuit Relations.

Michigan Pioneer and Historical Collections.

MOOREHEAD, WARREN K. The Stone Age in North America. Houghton Mifflin Co., Boston and New York, 1910.

OGBURN, WILLIAM FIELDING. Social Change. B.W. Huebsch, Inc., New York, 1922.

PARKER, A.C. The Archaeological History of New York. New York State Museum Bulletin, Nos. 235, 236, Albany, 1922.

SAWYER, ALVAH L. A History of the Northern Peninsula of Michigan. Lewis Publishing Co., Chicago, 1911.

SCHOOLCRAFT, HENRY R. Indian Tribes of the United States. Bureau of Indian Affairs. J.B. Lippincott and Co., Philadelphia, 1851-55.

SHETRONE, H.C. The Indian in Ohio. Ohio Archaeological and Historical Publications. Vol. 27. Columbus, 1919.

SMITH, HARLAN I. Memoranda Towards a Bibliography of the Archaeology of Michigan. Publication 10, Biological Series 3, Mich. Geol. and Biol. Survey, Lansing, 1912.

State Archaeological Surveys, Suggestions in Method and Technique. National Research Council, Washington, 1923.

WILDER, HARRIS H. Man's Prehistoric Past. Macmillan Co., New York, 1923.

Wisconsin Archaeologist.

WISSLER, CLARK. The American Indian. 2nd Edition. Oxford University Press, New York, 1922.

REFERENCES CITED AND CONSULTED - KRAKKER

BOAS, FRANZ. Review of Roland B. Dixon, The Racial History of Man. Science 57:587-590, 1923.

DIXON, ROLAND B. The Racial History of Man. Charles Scribner's Sons, New York, 1923.

DUSTIN, FRED. A Summary of the Archaeology of Isle Royale, Michigan. Papers, Mich. Acad. Sci. Arts and Letters 16:1-16, 1932.

Report on the Indian Earthworks in Ogamaw County, Michigan. Cranbrook Institute of Science, Scientific Publications 1. Bloomfield Hills, 1932.

Some Pioneers of Michigan Archaeology. Michigan History Magazine 20:213-219, 1936.

Editor of the Michigan Alumnus. University Makes Survey of Isle Royale. Michigan Alumnus 37:28, 33, 1930.

FOX, GEORGE R. What About Michigan Archaeology? Michigan History Magazine 6:415-434, 1922.

Isle Royale Expedition. Michigan History Magazine 13:306-323, 1929.

GILLMAN, HENRY. Certain Characteristics Pertaining to Ancient Man in Michigan. Smithsonian Institution, Annual Report, 1875 pp. 234-245. Washington, D.C., 1876.

GREENMAN, EMERSON F. A Report on Michigan Archaeology. American Anthropologist 28:310-313, 1926.

Michigan Mounds with Special Reference to Two in Missaukee County. Papers, Mich. Acad. Sci. Arts and Letters 7:1-9, 1927.

The Younge Site: An Archaeological Record from Michigan. Occasional Contributions from the Museum of Anthropology of the University of Michigan 6, 1937.

Wilbert B. Hinsdale, Michigan's Prehistorian. Michigan History 29: 189-197, 1945.

GRIFFIN, JAMES B. The Museum of Anthropology. In The University of Michigan: An Encylopedic Survey, edited by Walter A. Donnely, pp. 1476-1481. University of Michigan, 1958.

GUTHE, CARL E. Museum Growth is Interesting Story. Michigan Alumnus 36:211-214, 1929.

Archaeological Field Work in North America During 1929: Michigan. American Anthropologist 32:356, 1930.

Makes a Profession of a Hobby. Michigan Alumnus 37:387-388, 1931.

Reports, Archaeological Field Work in North America During 1931: Michigan. American Anthropologist 34:493, 1932.

HAIGHT, FLOYD L. Isle Royale Our New National Park. Michigan History 30:675-679, 1946.

HINSDALE, BURKE A. History of the University of Michigan, edited by Isaac N. Demmon. University of Michigan, 1906.

HINSDALE, WILBERT B. The Missaukee Preserve and Rifle River Forts. Papers, Mich. Acad. Sci. Arts and Letters 4(1):1-12, 1925a.

An Unusual Trephined Skull from Michigan. Papers, Mich. Acad. Sci. Arts and Letters 4(1):13-14, 1925b.

Notes on State Archaeological Surveys During 1924: Michigan. American Anthropologist 27:584-585, 1925c.

Archaeological Work by State Agencies, 1925: Michigan. American Anthropologist 28:681-682, 1926a.

Religion at the Algonquin Level. Papers, Mich. Acad. Sci. Arts and Letters 5:15-27, 1926b.

Archaeological Field Work in North America During 1926: Michigan. American Anthropologist 29(2):316-317, 1927a.

The Indians of Washtenaw County. George Wahr, Ann Arbor, 1927b.

Indian Modes of Travel in Michigan: Waterways. Papers, Mich. Acad. Sci. Arts and Letters 7:11-20, 1927c.

Reports, Archaeological Field Work in North America During 1927: Michigan. American Anthropologist 30:509-511, 1928a.

Indian Corn Culture in Michigan. Papers, Mich. Acad. Sci. Arts and Letters 8:31-49, 1928b.

Archaeological Field Work in North America During 1928: Michigan. American Anthropologist 31:348-349, 1929a.

Indian Mounds, West Twin Lake, Montmorency County, Michigan. Papers, Mich. Acad. Sci. Arts and Letters 10:91-101, 1929b.

Reports on Archaeological Field Work in the Summer of 1928 in Montmorency, Newaygo and Lake Counties, Michigan. Papers, Mich. Acad. Sci. Arts and Letters 12:127-135, 1930a.

The First People of Michigan. George Wahr, Ann Arbor, 1930b.

Spirit Stones. Papers, Mich. Acad. Sci Arts and Letters 14:103-112, 1931a.

Archaeological Atlas of Michigan. University of Michigan Museums, Michigan Handbook Series 4. University of Michigan Press, 1931b.

Distribution of the Aboriginal Population of Michigan. Occasional Contributions from the Museum of Anthropology of the University of Michigan 2, 1932a.

The Beginning of Pharmacy. The Journal of the American Institute of Homeopathy. pp. 41-50, 1932b.

Tecumseh's Illusions. Papers, Mich. Acad. Sci. Arts and Letters 18:31-52, 1933.

Perforated Skulls: An Inquiry. Wisconsin Archaeologist 14:37, 1934.

Archaeological Field Work in North America During 1934: Michigan. American Antiquity 1:113-114, 1935.

HINSDALE, WILBERT B. AND STEPHEN C. CAPPANNARI. Distribution of Perforated Human Crania in the Western Hemisphere. Papers, Mich. Acad. Sci. Arts and Letters 26:459-462, 1941.

HINSDALE, WILBERT B. AND EMERSON F. GREENMAN. Perforated

Indian Crania in Michigan. Occasional Contributions from the Museum of Anthropology of the University of Michigan 5, 1936.

HOLMES, W.H.   Handbook of Aboriginal American Antiquities, Part I, Introduction, The Lithic Industries. Smithsonian Institution, Bureau of American Ethnology, Bulletin 60, 1919.

HRDLICKA, ALES.   Skeletal Remains Suggesting or Attributed to Early Man in North America. Smithsonian Institution, Bureau of American Ethnology, Bulletin 33, 1907.

MILLS, WILLIAM C.   Archaeological Atlas of Ohio. Ohio State Archaeological and Historical Society, Columbus, 1914.

SMITH, HARLAN I.   Archaeological Survey of Michigan. American Anthropologist 3:198-200, 1901.

The Antiquities of Michigan, Their Value and Impending Loss. Michigan Pioneer and Historical Collections 31:238-252, 1902.

Preliminary List of the Sites of Aboriginal Remains in Michigan. Michigan Geological and Biological Survey, Publication 1, Biological Series 1, 1910.

STARR, FREDERICK.   Perforated Skulls from Michigan. The American Antiquarian and Oriental Journal 12:165-166, 1890.

STEVENS, EDWARD J.   Michigan State Archaeological Survey. Michigan History Magazine 11:436-444, 1927.

WILLEY, GORDON R., AND JEREMY A. SABLOFF. A History of American Archaeology (second ed.). W.H. Freeman and Co., San Francisco, 1980.

PLATE I

Figure 1.   Great Mound at River Rouge, height 40 feet.   From Hubbard, Memorials of a Half-Century   Totally destroyed.

Figure 2.   Mounds on bank of Grand River, height 15 feet. Kent County.

PLATE I

1

2

PLATE II

Base map of Michigan with number of authenticated mounds in each county indicated. 1924.

PLATE II

PLATE III

Figure 1. Inclosure on the Missaukee Preserve. Greatest diameter 177 feet, height of embankment about 5 feet, width of embankment on top about 7 feet. Cross-section below.

Figure 2. Inclosure on the Missaukee Preserve. Greatest diameter 156 feet, height about 5 feet, width of embankment on top about 7 feet. Distance from Figure 1, 30 rods. Cross-section below.

PLATE III

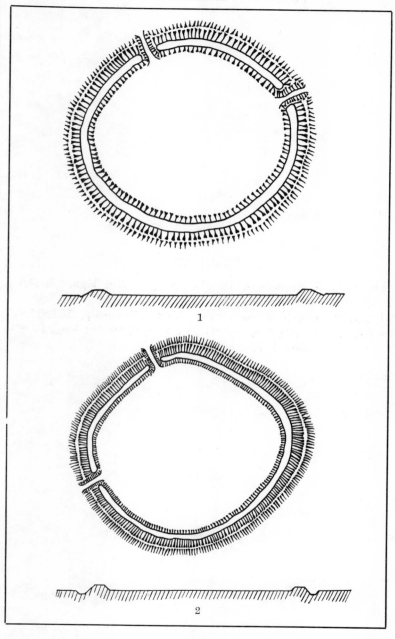

1

2

PLATE IV

Figure 1. Embankment, 450 feet long, 3 feet high. Reider Township, Missaukee County.

Figure 2. Group of earthworks, Reider Township, Missaukee County. A. 110 feet long, B. 251 feet long, C. 80 feet long, D. 92 feet long. Average 3 feet in height.

PLATE IV

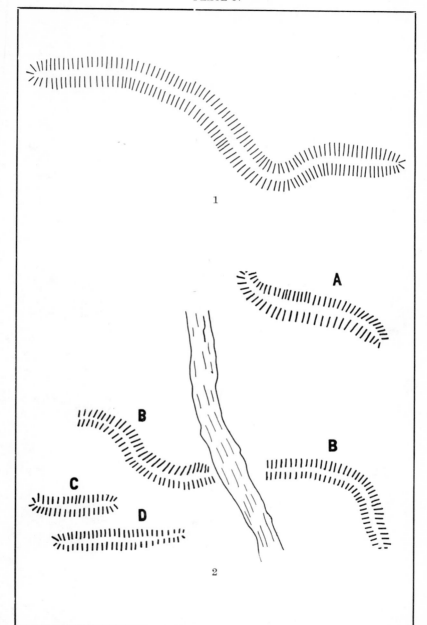

PLATE V

Figure 1.   Rifle River Fort No. 3 : a, b, c, and d, original openings in walls of fort;e-f opening probably made by lumbermen.
Figure 2.   Rifle River Fort No. 4, Ogemaw County.

PLATE V

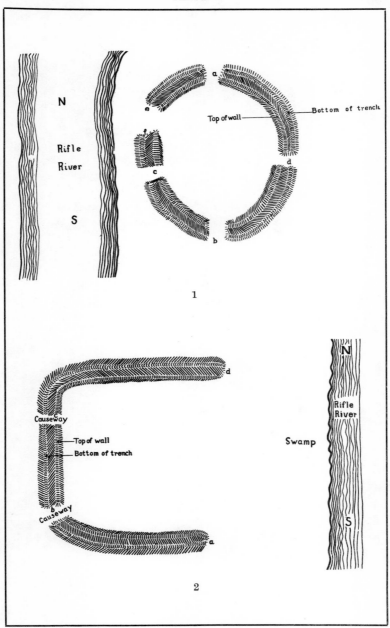

1

2

PLATE VI

Ancient Earthworks, Macomb County, on Clinton River. From Hubbard, Memorials of a Half-Century.

PLATE VI

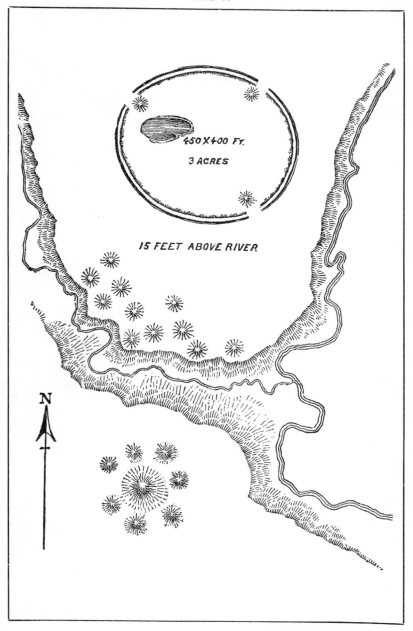

450 X 400 Ft.

3 ACRES

15 FEET ABOVE RIVER

N

PLATE VII

Diagrammatic sketches of ancient garden beds near Kalamazoo.

PLATE VII

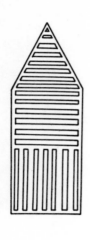

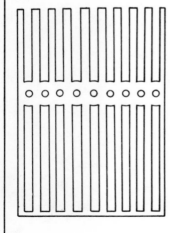

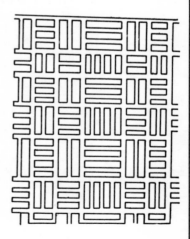

PLATE VIII

Figure 1. Skull with arrow embedded in left orbit. From grave in Lenawee County.

Figure 2. Trephined skull from Devil River Mound, Alpena County. Healing well advanced.

PLATE VIII

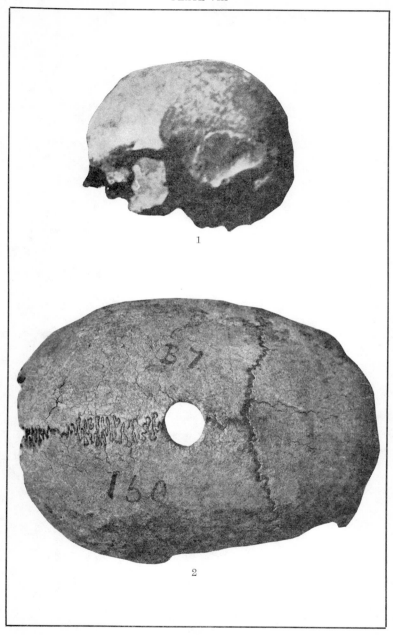

1

2

PLATE IX

Various forms of Michigan flints; arrows and spears.

PLATE IX

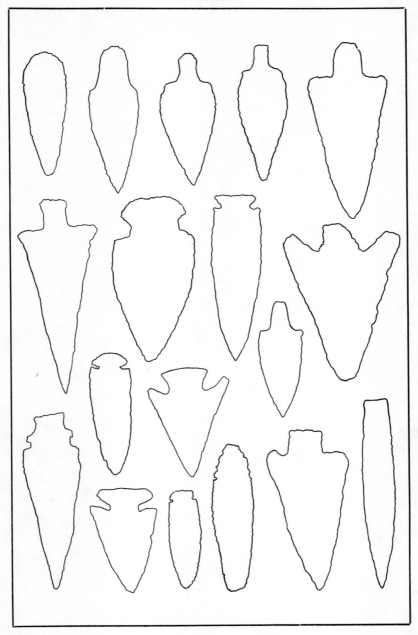

PLATE X

Various forms of Michigan flints; arrows, spears, knives, scrap-ers and drills.

PLATE X

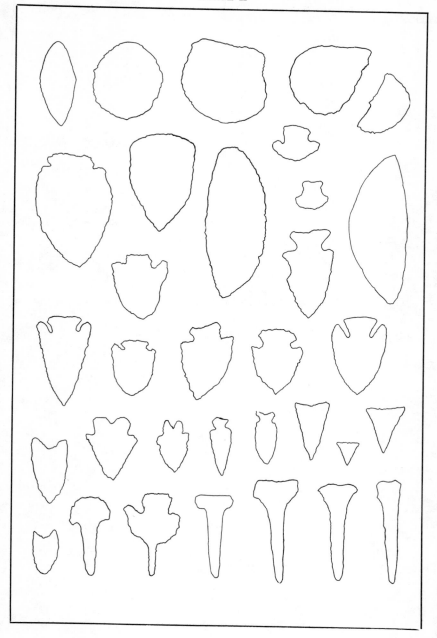

PLATE XI

Figure 1. Double grooved adze, length 2¼ inches. Washtenaw County.

Figure 2. Double bitted axe about 8 inches long. Lenawee County. From Moorehead, Stone Age in North America.

Figure 3. Gouge, hard stone, length 11 inches. Washtenaw County.

Figure 4. Mauls and hammers, weight varying from 12 pounds to 13 ounces. Largest from Lake Superior copper mines.

PLATE XI

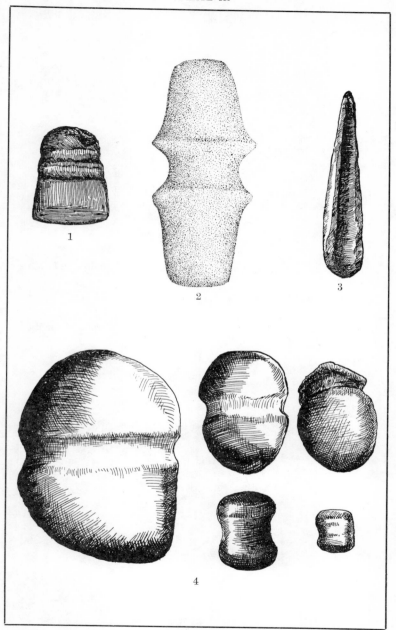

PLATE XII

Figure 1. Double grooved maul, length 6¼ inches. Branch County.

Figure 2. Double grooved axe, length 4½ inches. Calhoun County.

Figure 3. Axe with wide slanting groove, length 8 inches. Mackinaw County.

Figure 4. Fluted axe, length 10 inches. Charlevoix County.

PLATE XII

1

2

3

4

PLATE XIII

Figure 1.   Granite chisel, length 6 inches.   Washtenaw County.

Figure 2.   Granite hatchet, length 6 inches.   Washtenaw County.

Figure 3.   Granite hatchet, length 7 inches.   Washtenaw County.

Figure 4.   Double bitted, wide grooved axe, length 6 inches. Washtenaw County.

Figure 5.   Side view of axe shown on frontispiece, length 9½ inches, weight 4¾ pounds.   Lapeer County.

PLATE XIII

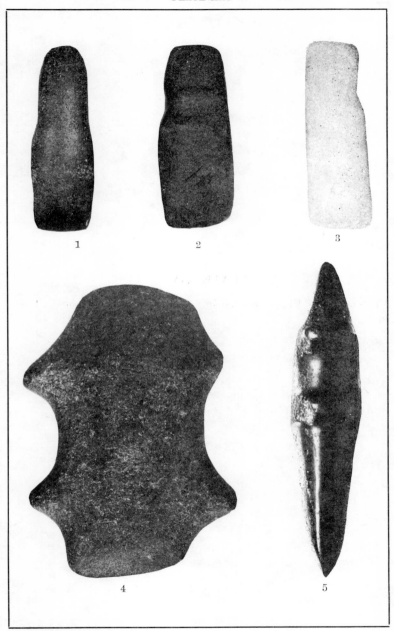

1   2   3

4   5

PLATE XIV

'Totem' axe. Figure pecked in. Length about 5 inches Tuscola County.

PLATE XIV

PLATE XV

Fluted celt, length 8 inches. Bay County. Fluting on one side only.

PLATE XV

PLATE XVI

Figure 1. Banded slate butterfly stone. Michigan.

Figure 2. Mottled granite, perforation partly bored. Washtenaw County.

Figure 3. Pendants and gorgets of various forms. Washtenaw County.

PLATE XVI

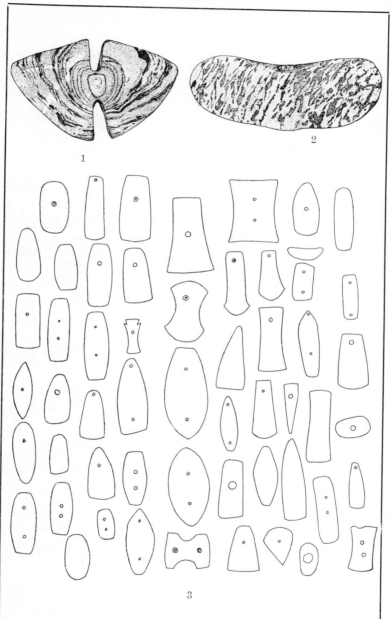

1

2

3

PLATE XVII

Figure 1. Slate spud, length 8¾ inches. Kent Scientific Museum.

Figure 2. Double bitted axe-shaped ceremonial of banded slate, length 4 inches. Washtenaw County.

Figure 3. Banded slate, width 6 inches. Washtenaw County.

Figure 4. Double crescents about 7 inches long. Upper from Jackson County, lower from Wayne County.

Figure 5. Crescent banner stones. Second from bottom from Shiawassee County, others from Eaton County.

PLATE XVII

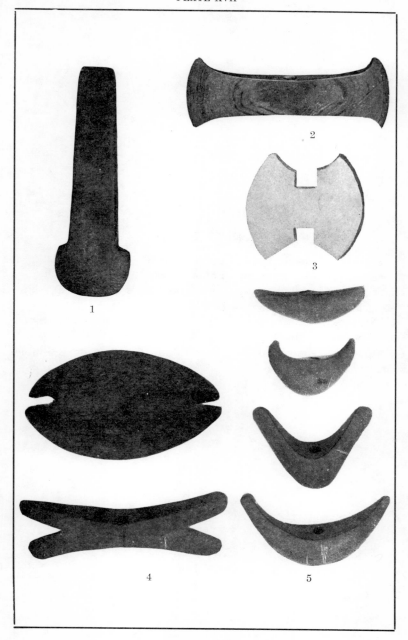

PLATE XVIII

Figure 1. Banner stone. Eaton County.

Figure 2. Banner stone. Eaton County.

Figure 3. Double crescent ceremonial of green banded slate, 6½ x 4 inches, restored. Jackson County.

Figure 4. Ceremonial, length 5½ inches. Isabella County. Kent Scientific Museum.

Figure 5. Unfinished broken slate, 6 inches wide. Clinton County.

PLATE XVIII

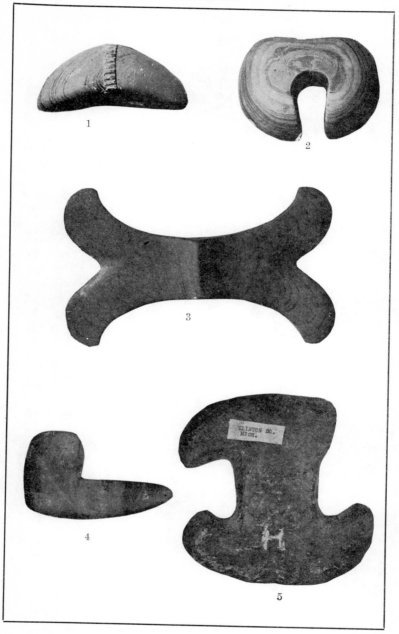

PLATE XIX

Figure 1.   Objects loaned by various collectors.   Michigan.
Figure 2.   Plummet, tube, bar amulet and hatchet; loaned by various collectors.   Michigan.
Figure 3.   Miscellaneous collection of stone and slate objects, mostly ceremonials.   Michigan.

PLATE XIX

1

2

3

PLATE XX

Figure 1. Bird-stone. Bay County.
Figure 2. Problematical object.
Figure 3. Problematical object, slate tube.
Figure 4. Banded slate bird-stone, length 4 inches. Kent County. Kent Scientific Museum.
Figure 5. Bird-stone. Washtenaw County.
Figure 6. Bird-stone. Washtenaw County.
Figure 7. Bird-stone. Genesee County.

PLATE XX

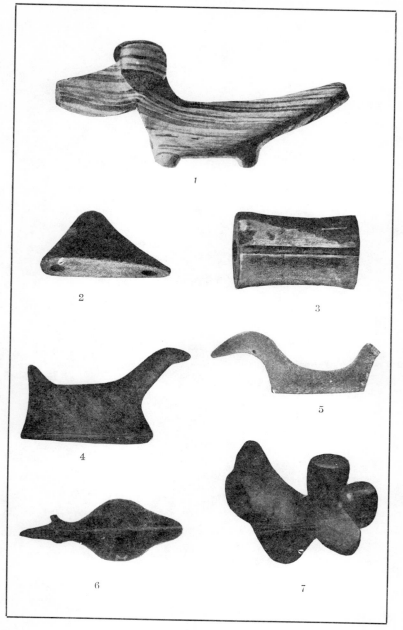

1

2

3

4

5

6

7

PLATE XXI

Figure 1.   Bird-stone, perforations for eyes, and tally notches along back and markings on side.   Washtenaw County.

Figure 2.   Banded slate, length 7 inches.   Kent County.   Kent Scientific Museum.

Figure 3.   Bird-stones.   Eaton County.

PLATE XXI

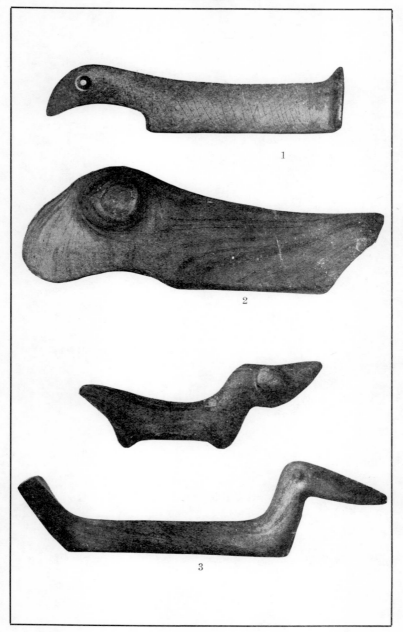

1

2

3

PLATE XXII

Figure 1. Crude stone pipes from grave. Saline, Washtenaw County.

Figure 2. 'Micmac' pipes. Washtenaw County.

Figure 3. Fine grained granite pipe. Washtenaw County.

Figure 4. Heavy clay pipe, length 5½ inches, found 2 feet below the surface. Missaukee County.

Figure 5. Fine grained granite pipe, length 2½ inches. Washtenaw County.

PLATE XXII

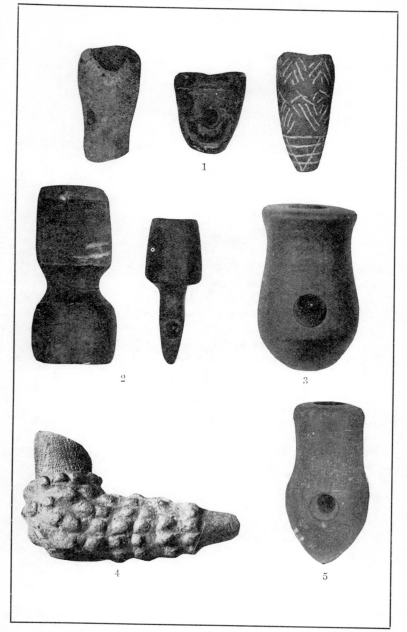

PLATE XXIII

Figure 1. Platform pipe, length 4½ inches on base. Kent County. Kent Scientific Museum.

Figure 2. Tubular pipe of banded slate. Boring 'funneled' to small opening at flattened end. Ingham County.

Figure 3. Funnel shaped pipe of gray sandstone. 'Funnel' inside tapers to opening at small end. Ingham County.

Figure 4. Frog pipe. Eaton County.

PLATE XXIII

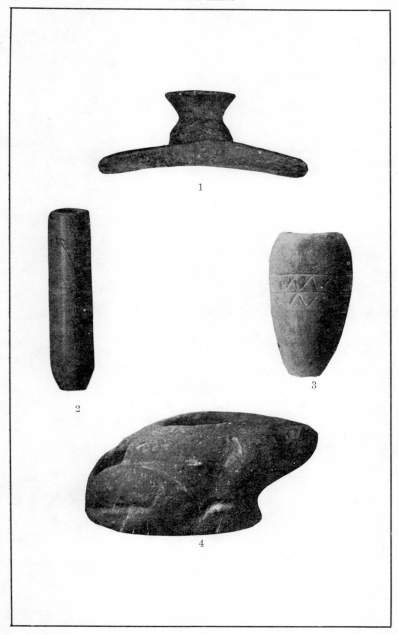

1

2

3

4

PLATE XXIV

Four aspects of turtle pipe, length 4 inches.   Oakland County.

PLATE XXIV

PLATE XXV

Figure 1.   Bell shaped pestle.   Alpena County.
Figure 2.   Bell shaped pestle.   Alpena County.
Figure 3.   Various pestles, length from 5 to 21 inches.   Michigan.

PLATE XXV

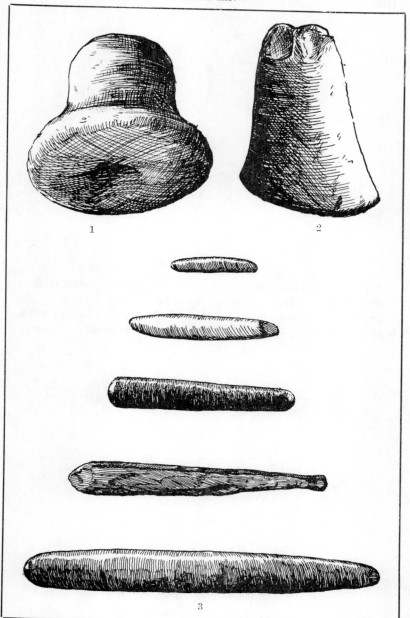

1

2

3

PLATE XXVI

Figure 1.   Shallow mortar, diameter 7 inches.   Indentation on opposite side.   Alpena County, Michigan.

Figure 2.   Pitted stone, 7 inches in diameter, 4 inches thick: 6 pits on one side, 7 on the other.   Washtenaw County, Michigan.

PLATE XXVI

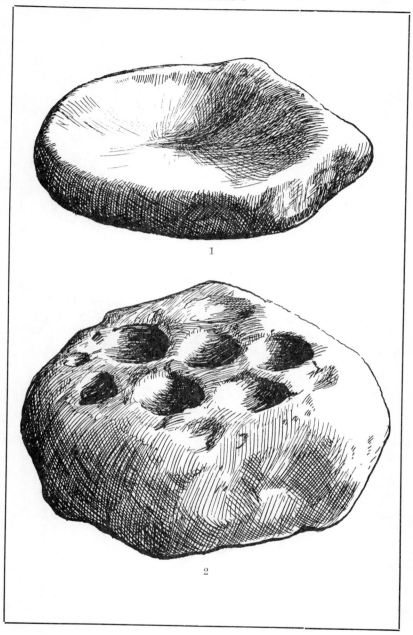

1

2

PLATE XXVII

Figure 1.   Mortar, weight 30 pounds.   St. Joseph County.
Figure 2.   Mortar, weight 47½ pounds.   Jackson County.

PLATE XXVII

1

2

PLATE XXVIII

Figure 1. Pots from mounds near Grand Rapids. From Hubbard, Memorials of a Half-Century.

Figure 2. Clay bowl. Kent County Mounds.

Figure 3. Clay bowl, Norton Mounds. Kent County.

Figure 4. Clay bowl. Kent County Mounds.

PLATE XXVIII

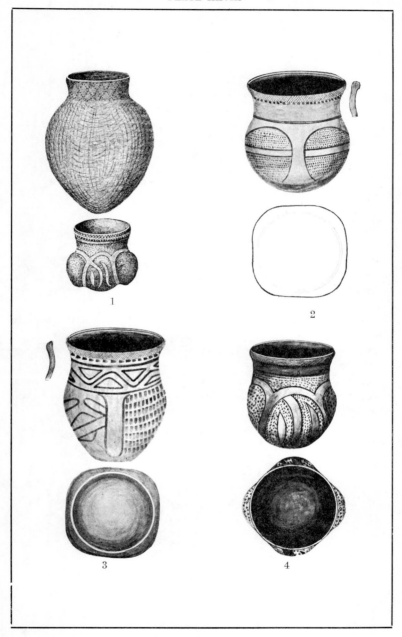

1

2

3

4

PLATE XXIX

Figure 1. Copper hook, length 6 inches.

Figure 2. Copper spear head, length 14 inches.   Ontonagon County.

Figure 3. Copper spear head, length 4½ inches. Copper Falls Mine.

Figure 4. Copper gad, length 4 inches.   Minnesota mine, Michigan.

Figure 5. Copper implement, length 6½ inches.   Isabella County.

Figure 6. Copper chisel, length 13 inches. Ontonagon County.

Figure 7. Copper chisel, length 7 inches.

Figure 8. Side view of Figure 7.

All, except Figure 5, from Whittlesey, Ancient Mining on the Shores of Lake Superior.

PLATE XXIX

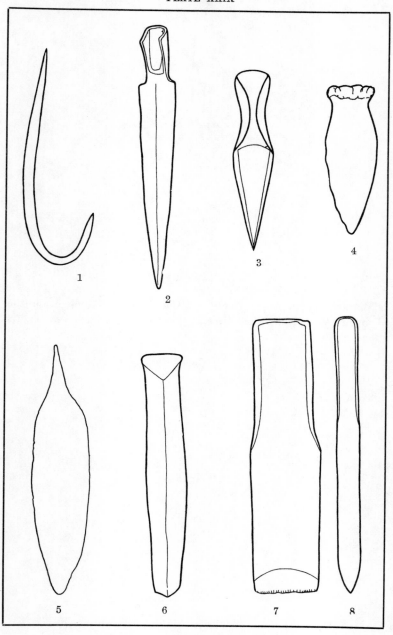

PLATE XXX

Worked copper from Michigan.   Collection of Claude Hamilton,
Grand Rapids.

PLATE XXX

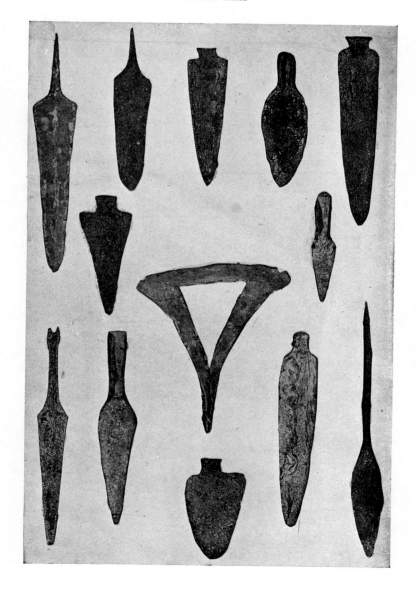

PLATE XXXI

Figure 1. Copper tools and spear. Michigan.

Figure 2. Piece of float copper weighing 484 pounds. This presents a striking resemblance to a human profile. The edges about the mouth and nose appear to have been folded back to bring out the features more strikingly. Greatest diameter 40 inches. Keweenaw Peninsula.

Figure 3. Rows of pits from which prehistoric workmen have mined copper. Triangle Island, Lake Superior.

PLATE XXXI

1

2

3

PLATE XXXII

Figure 1.　Marine shell dipper, 11 x 5½ inches.　Kent Scientific Museum.

Figure 2.　Marine shell gorget.　Saline, Michigan.

Figure 3.　Pendants, 10 and 7 inches long, made from cores of large marine shells.　Taken from grave, Isabella County.

Figure 4.　Marine shell drinking vessel, 5 x 7 inches.　From Indian grave, Oceana County.

PLATE XXXII

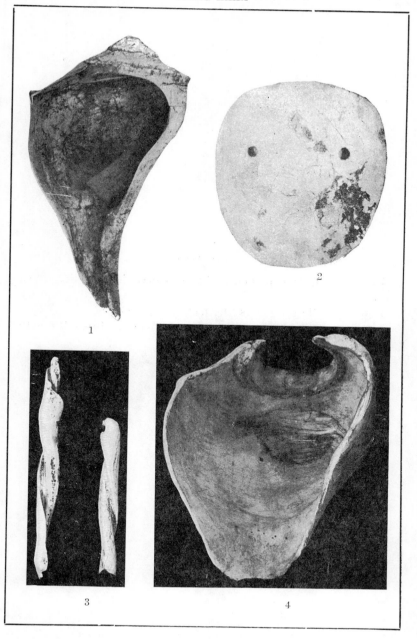

PLATE XXXIII

Figure 1.   Runtee, probably of fossil ivory. Natural size. Wexford County.

Figure 2.   Perforated pestle, length 5¾ inches.

Figure 3.   Pots from mound, Wayne County.   From Hubbard, Memorials of a Half-Century.

PLATE XXXIII

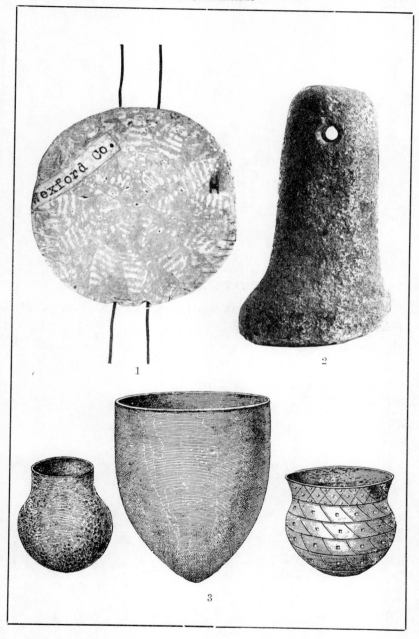

1

2

3

PLATE XXXIV

Rose and white flint, length 9½ inches. Kent County. Kent Scientific Museum.

PLATE XXXIV

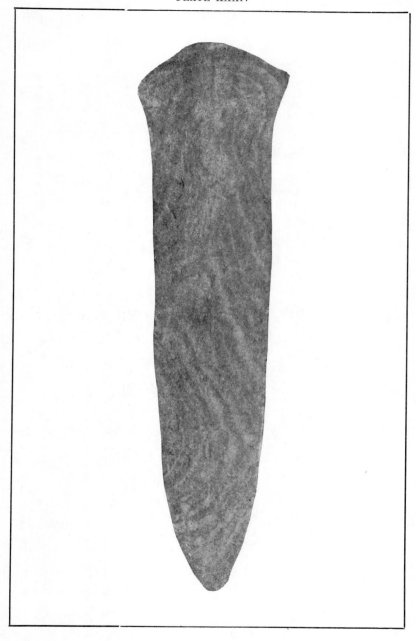

PLATE XXXV

Copper tool, length 8 inches. Washtenaw County.

PLATE XXXV

PLATE XXXVI

Figure 1. Butterfly stone with ridges and groove instead of hole through center. Genessee County.

Figure 2. Slate boat stone, perforation near each end. Surface find, Tuscola County.

Figure 3. Pipe of fine grained gray stone. Plowed up, Tuscola County.

PLATE XXXVI

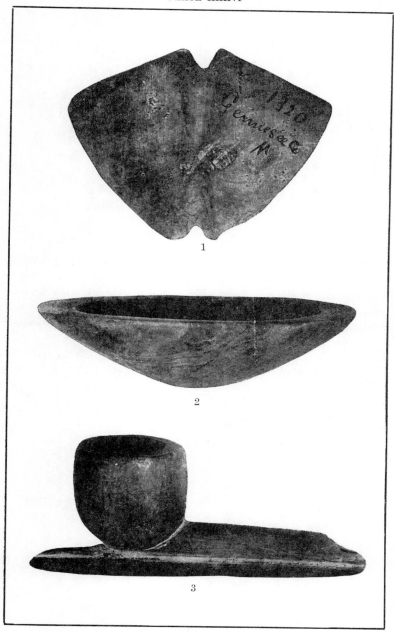

1

2

3

PLATE XXXVII

Figure 1. Bone implements, 7 and 10 inches long. Kent County mound.

Figure 2. Walrus bone, taken from gravel pit with human bones. Standish.

Figure 3. Implement of elk bone, taken with human remains from excavation, Detroit, 1889.

Figure 4. Implement of bison bone, taken with human remains from excavation, Detroit, 1889.

PLATE XXXVII

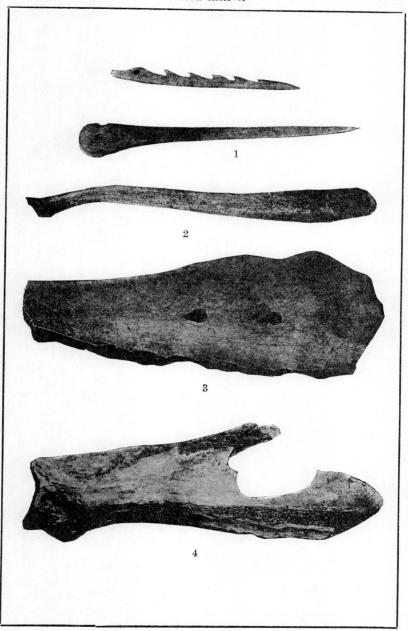

PLATE XXXVIII

Suggested method of using pestle. From Schoolcraft.

PLATE XXXVIII

PLATE XXXIX

Figure 1.   Bevelled arrow head of white flint.   Calhoun County.
Figure 2.   Tubular pipe of light sandstone, length 4 inches.
Bay County.
Figure 3.   Rock painting in cave near Manistique.

PLATE XXXIX

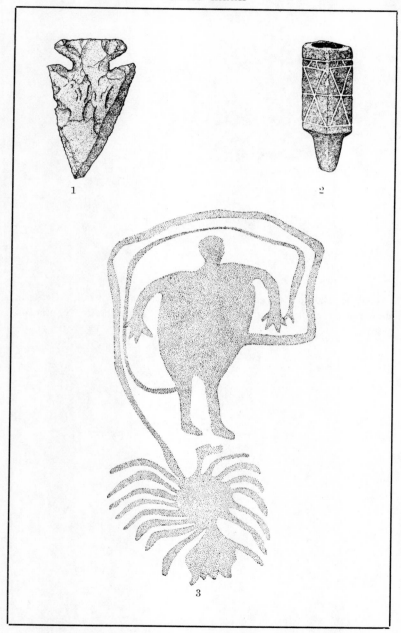

1

2

3

PLATE XL

Indian skeleton taken from gravel bank, Tecumseh, Michigan, showing by the silver ornaments contact with the early missionaries.

PLATE XL

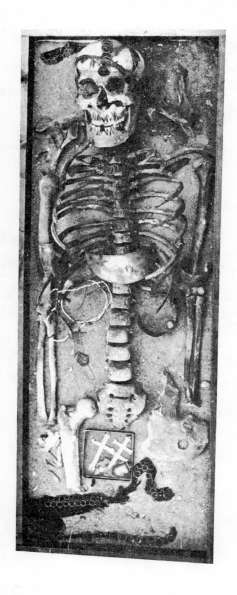

PLATE XLI

Figure 1. Old baskets, bead and tendon work, of Chippewa Indians.

Figure 2. Showing construction of the dome shaped lodge. From Bushnell.

PLATE XLI

1

2

SUGGESTED FURTHER READING

The literature of Michigan archaeology has expanded greatly with research done since Hinsdale's time. The following publications will be a useful beginning for readers who wish to explore Michigan prehistory further and study its native inhabitants.

Many libraries subscribe to *Michigan History,* which from time to time has articles concerning archaeology. In addition, the Michigan History Division publishes a pamphlet series called *Great Lakes Informant* which includes several pamphlets concerning archaeology. These are available by writing the Michigan History Division, Michigan Department of State, Lansing, Michigan, 48918.

Many libraries also receive the *Michigan Archaeologist,* the publication of the Michigan Archaeological Society. Each issue has current information on how to become a member of the society and receive the *Michigan Archaeologist.*

The following books are widely available in libraries. If your library does not have one ask your librarian about interlibrary loan. Some are available in inexpensive paperback editions which your local bookstore may carry in stock or may order for you.

Fitting, James E. *The Archaeology of Michigan: A guide to the Prehistory of the Great Lakes Region* (second ed.). Cranbrook Institute of Science, Bloomfield Hills, Michigan, 1975. (available in paperback)

Fitting reviews the archaeological work in Michigan through the 1960s. The book is somewhat out of date now since the text was not revised when the new edition was issued, but it is still a good survey of Michigan prehistory for the reader with a limited archaeological background.

Kinietz, W. Vernon. *The Indians of the Western Great Lakes: 1615-1760.* University of Michigan Press, Ann Arbor, 1965. (available in paperback)

This book is a good beginning for the study of Great Lakes ethnohistory. Many sources are utilized that would probably not be easily available to the average reader.

Mason, Ronald J. *Great Lakes Archaeology.* Academic Press, New York, 1981.

This is the most recent review of Great Lakes prehistory. The text is directed toward the general reader and provides a broad regional view.

Trigger, Bruce G. (editor). *Handbook of North American Indians, Vol. 15, Northeast.* Smithsonian Institution, Washington, D.C., 1978.

Various chapters are relevant to Michigan prehistory and Indian groups. The volume contains good, brief summaries and provides many references for further study.

Quimby, George I. *Indian Life in the Upper Great Lakes.* University of Chicago Press, 1960. (available in paperback)

This is a good introduction for the beginner. Unfortunately the text is now somewhat out of date.